animals

animals

20 jewelry and accessory designs

by Tansy Wilson

First published 2014 by
Guild of Master Craftsman Publications Ltd
Castle Place, 166 High Street, Lewes,
East Sussex BN7 1XU

Text, designs, and illustrations
© Tansy Wilson, 2014
Copyright in the Work © GMC Publications Ltd, 2014

ISBN 978 1 86108 971 7

A catalog record for this book is available
from the British Library.

Set in King and Myriad
Color origination by GMC Reprographics
Printed and bound in China

Publisher Jonathan Bailey
Production Manager Jim Bulley
Managing Editor Gerrie Purcell
Senior Project Editor Dominique Page
Editor Ruth O'Rourke-Jones
Managing Art Editor Gilda Pacitti
Designer Rob Janes
Photographer Andrew Perris

contents

Continued...

KITTY

MARINA

CHICHI

The Projects

SPIKE

FENTON

RENARD

TEMBO

KAA

LEO

BUBBLES

CHIMPSKY

OCTAVIA

OPO

GECKO

SONIA

HARTLEY

SKYE

FLUTTERBY

RIBBIT

CLAUDIA

Tools

HAVING THE RIGHT TOOLS TO HAND MAKES TACKLING ANY TASK SIMPLER. WITH THE BASIC KIT ON THIS LIST, YOU SHOULD FIND MAKING ANY OF THE PIECES OF JEWELRY IN THIS BOOK A BREEZE!

pliers

When it comes to holding, forming, or shaping pieces of jewelry, the most common tools used are pliers. There are different types designed to suit particular tasks, but even if you have just one pair of multi pliers you should be able to tackle most projects.

ROUND-NOSE PLIERS

These pliers have round tapered jaws that are narrow at the tip, broadening to the base. They are used for shaping wire, wrapping loops, and making eyepins (see page 27).

FLAT-NOSE PLIERS

With flat parallel jaws at the top and bottom, these pliers are useful for bending sharp corners or straightening wire, closing flat ribbon crimps and holding, opening, or closing jumprings (see page 25) and other small components.

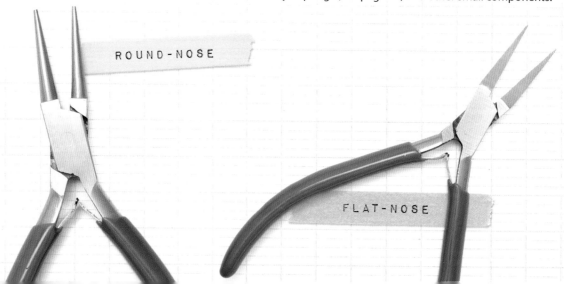

ROUND-NOSE

FLAT-NOSE

SNIPE-NOSE PLIERS

Sometimes known as chain-nose pliers, these pliers have half-round jaws with flat parallel inside faces that touch. They taper from a narrow tip to a wider half round at the base. Their unique shape makes them ideal for holding small jewelry components, opening and closing chain links, and shaping wire in general.

CRIMPING PLIERS

Crimping pliers come in a variety of sizes and it is important to have the correct size jaw for the crimps that you use most often. The jaw has two sections: the back forms your crimp tube into a curve, trapping the contents, while the front folds the crimp in half securing everything in place.

MULTI PLIERS

This pair of pliers combines the functions of the flat-nose pliers and the round-nose pliers because the jaws change shape half way down. They have a cutting surface on them too—making them an ideal pair of pliers for first-time makers!

MULTI-SIZED LOOPING PLIERS /WIRE-WRAP MANDRELS

With many sizes of round jaws on one surface, these pliers enable you to make jumprings and loops to a certain size. Wire-wrap mandrels are usually a less expensive option of the same tool that can do the job just as well.

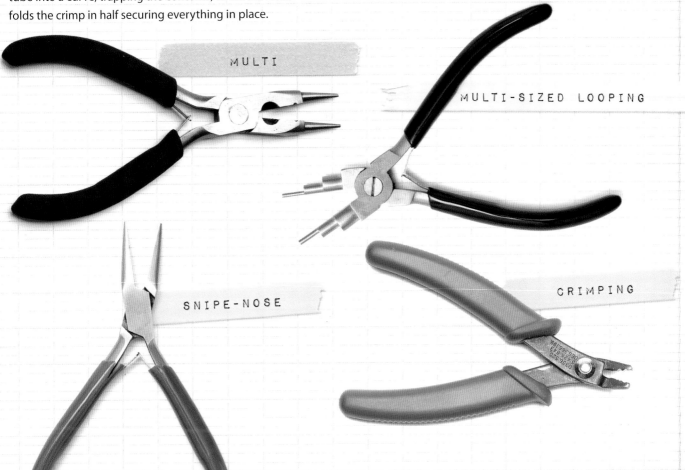

MULTI

MULTI-SIZED LOOPING

SNIPE-NOSE

CRIMPING

cutters

A variety of different types and sizes of cutter are used in making jewelry. Top and side cutters are used for cutting thin materials and wire, while heavier-duty pliers or memory-wire cutters are used for thicker wire. You probably already have a pair of scissors to use for cutting paper or fabric, though a craft knife makes a good alternative.

TOP CUTTERS

The cutting surface on this tool is at the very top, as the name suggests. Materials such as wire can be cut at 90 degrees, extremely close and flush to your piece.

SIDE CUTTERS

These work in a similar way to top cutters but with the cutting surface on the side of the tool. The nose is slightly tapered, giving you access to smaller areas in your work.

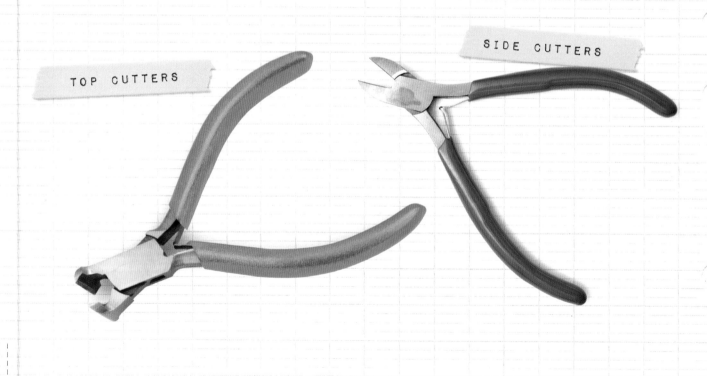

TOP CUTTERS

SIDE CUTTERS

HEAVY-DUTY OR MEMORY-WIRE CUTTERS

These are a heavier-duty pair of cutters used for cutting memory wire or thicker-gauge wire. Using these cutters will keep the blades on your side or top cutters sharp and dent-free.

SCISSORS AND CRAFT KNIFE

You can use general-purpose scissors for your jewelry projects but make sure they have a fine, long nose so that you can accurately cut fabric and paper. A craft knife is handy for getting into those trickier curved designs and small places where scissors may be more awkward.

PIERCING SAW AND BLADES

This tool uses separate saw blades for cutting wire, tube, and sheet metal. It gives a clean cut without marking the surface at all. Piercing saws are ideal for making jumprings as they cut the wire completely flush without leaving an indent. This ensures that the jumprings close nice and tightly.

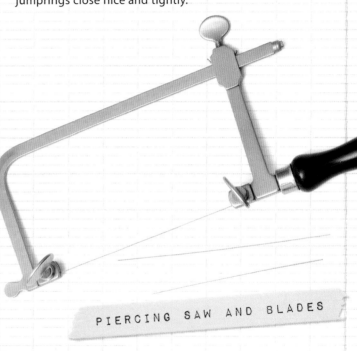

MEMORY-WIRE CUTTERS

PIERCING SAW AND BLADES

SCISSORS AND CRAFT KNIFE

other essentials

You may have some of these items stashed away around the house somewhere, so dig them out and make a new home for them in your jewelry toolbox.

RING MANDREL

This is a tapered cylindrical former with measurements marked evenly along it that correspond to ring sizes. Place one of your existing rings onto it to see what size your finger is. Wrap wire at this point to guarantee a ring that fits you perfectly.

DRILL BIT

Drill bits come in many sizes and are normally inserted into an electric or hand drill for making holes. Alternatively, you can twist them by hand through soft materials.

BEAD BOARD

This is a great tool for planning the length of necklaces. The channels have measurements on them and by placing your beads in the channels you can see exactly how many you will need. The compartments in the middle are for holding the findings that you will be using for that particular piece.

BEAD MAT

A cheaper equivalent to the bead board, this cushioned soft mat stops your beads and findings from rolling around. It does not have any compartments in it.

BEADING NEEDLE

A beading needle is made from extremely fine wire formed into a needle shape. What makes it special is that the "eye" collapses, enabling you to string even the smallest of beads with ease.

RING MANDREL

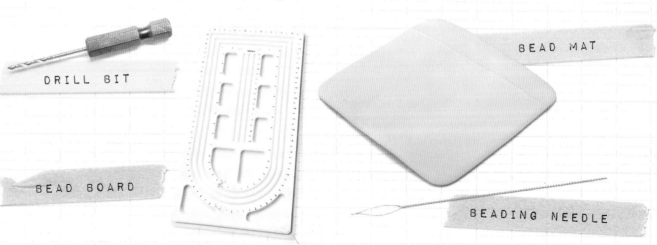

DRILL BIT

BEAD BOARD

BEAD MAT

BEADING NEEDLE

Animals

SEWING NEEDLES AND THREAD

You will need to sew components in place for some of the projects. It is always a good idea to keep a range of needles and different colored cottons in your toolkit.

ADHESIVE

A quick-setting adhesive, such as cyanoacrylate (superglue), is ideal for use on all types of beads and threads. Adding a drop onto knots also provides extra security.

Two-part adhesives mix together to form an adhesive of a thicker consistency. These are useful where you do not want glue to run onto other surfaces.

White (PVA) glue is great for painting onto surfaces as it dries completely clear and rigid. This makes it useful for stiffening fabrics or sealing papers prior to using resin.

Latex-based rubber cement (Copydex) is an ideal adhesive to stick absorbent materials together.

GLUE GUN

A glue gun heats up sticks of glue to melting point so that you can squeeze blobs of hot glue onto certain surfaces—such as metal and plastic—where other thinner adhesives may not be as effective. Be careful because the glue can get incredibly hot.

TAPE MEASURE OR RULER

Whether you are working with wire or fabric, a tape measure or ruler is essential for measuring your materials to obtain accurate lengths for your design.

MARKER PENS AND NAIL VARNISH

Marker pens—both normal and metallic—are easier to see when drawing measurements onto wire, nylon, or steel-coated threads than ordinary pen. Nail varnish can also be used, especially when coloring the ends of headpins to give a unique touch to any design.

MASKING TAPE

It is handy to have a roll of masking tape in your toolbox so you can add a piece of tape to hold glued surfaces together while drying, leaving you to carry on making.

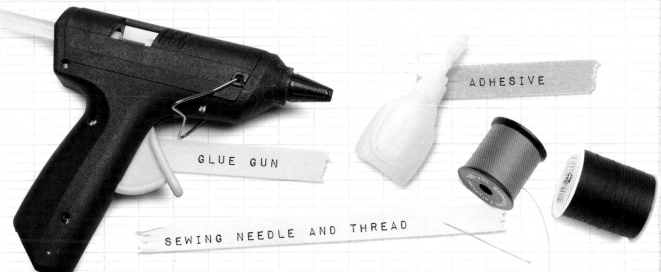

GLUE GUN

ADHESIVE

SEWING NEEDLE AND THREAD

Materials

THE SKY IS THE LIMIT WHEN SOURCING MATERIALS TO USE IN JEWELRY MAKING—ANYTHING GOES! FROM BASIC ESSENTIALS LIKE THREAD, WIRE, AND FINDINGS TO GLASS, FABRIC, OR HOMEMADE MODELING-CLAY BEADS. LET YOUR IMAGINATION RUN RIOT.

beads and charms

Be inspired by the huge variety of beads and charms that are available in a whole assortment of materials. Get creative by mixing up shapes, sizes, textures, and colors.

LUCITE BEADS

Lucite beads are made from a type of plastic. Their pretty colors, combined with variety of shapes and sizes make them a great bead for any design and they look particularly effective when clustered together.

SEED BEADS AND BUGLE BEADS

These are tiny glass beads that come in an enormous choice of colors and mixes. Seed beads are usually $1/32$–$1/8$in (1–2mm) round whereas bugle beads are thin tubes that can be as long as ½in (12mm) (see Sonia, page 94.)

LUCITE BEADS

SEED BEADS AND BUGLE BEADS

LAMPWORK BEADS

Glass lampwork beads are beautiful and great for giving your piece a focal point. To really let them stand out, try simply using them on their own for added impact.

CHARMS

As with general beads, there are zillions of different ones to buy. Working with a theme helps to decide which ones to use (see Fenton, page 50).

GENERAL BEADS

With so many beads to choose from, sometimes it's best to think of their character to inspire a design. Wooden beads look rustic and ethnic while crystals look more contemporary. Using cord-covered beads with fabric maintains a strong theme. Keep adding to your collection by buying your favorite colors and shapes and you'll find that design ideas just start to happen.

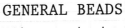

LAMPWORK BEADS

GENERAL BEADS

CHARMS

WHILE THE CONVERSIONS FROM METRIC TO IMPERIAL ARE AS ACCURATE AS POSSIBLE IT IS ALWAYS BEST TO STICK TO ONE SYSTEM OR THE OTHER THROUGHOUT A PROJECT.

Materials

stringing materials

Whatever design you choose, you will need to select a stringing material. From elastics and nylon threads to wires and chains, the right material will quite literally bring your creation together.

BEADING ELASTIC

This non-slippery elastic is made up of several strands, which makes it very easy to tie knots in. It can be prone to snapping so you may need to use extra lengths for doubling up when stringing.

NYLON THREAD

This thread is like a fishing line in that it is extremely strong and comes in many different gauges. Being strong yet fine makes it extremely versatile although it does not stretch at all. You can tie knots in it but I would advise adding a drop of glue to secure them.

NYLON-COATED WIRE

Often referred to as "TigerTail," this is constructed of several fine steel wires bound together in a nylon coating. It comes in many colors and thicknesses and is stronger than nylon but cannot be knotted. Ideally you should use crimps to add clasps or other findings.

BEADING ELASTIC

NYLON THREAD

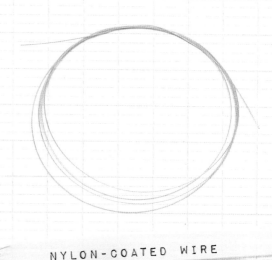

NYLON-COATED WIRE

MEMORY WIRE

This wire comes in different-sized coils that can be manipulated but always go back to their original size. It's a great wire to use for bangles as the coils can be sized to fit your wrist, meaning you don't need to use clasps.

WIRE

Wire comes in many different gauges and colors, making it extremely versatile for a wide range of projects. Using very fine wire wrapped around thicker wire adds an extra feature to your design.

CHAIN

Chain comes in an abundance of styles, sizes, and colors. You can use it as a real feature in a design (see Chimpsky, page 76) rather than just dangling a pendant from it.

MEMORY WIRE

CHAIN

WIRE

Materials

fabrics, ribbons, and feathers

Combining fabrics, ribbons, or feathers in your designs can create wonderful tactile pieces and is a great way to play with color or reinforce a theme.

FELT

You can buy felt sheets in almost any color you can think of. The unique thing about this fabric is that you can cut any shape with no danger of the edges fraying.

ORGANZA

This fabric—contrary to felt—frays excessively. You can use this feature to your advantage by purposefully fraying the edges to obtain a soft, wispy effect (see Leo, page 68).

PATTERNED FABRIC AND RIBBON

Whatever your design, you are sure to find a fabric or ribbon that will complement your idea.

FEATHERS

Feathers come in a variety of colors, sizes, and shapes. Some are even painted to look like butterflies (see Flutterby, page 108). You can also strip a feather to customize it to your desired size and shape by pulling the barbs away from the quill.

PATTERNED FABRIC AND RIBBON

FEATHERS

findings

All those little bits and pieces used in jewelry that hold your designs together are collectively known as findings. There's an array of ready-made findings available but why not try making some for yourself (see pages 25–29)?

HEADPINS AND EYEPINS

These are metal wires with a pinhead or an eye loop at one end. They are handy for threading and connecting beads together.

EARRING FINDINGS

I use both earring hooks and flat-back studs in this book. The hooks have an open loop at the bottom that you can connect and hang beads or chain from while the studs have a flat surface that you can glue a component directly onto.

EARRING CHANDELIER HOOPS

A chandeliers is a large decorative connector that hangs from an earring hook. You can thread beads directly onto it or buy ones that have many loops to hang beads from.

JUMPRINGS

A jumpring is a single ring of metal that is used mainly to join or link pieces together. You close the ring to secure the item in place.

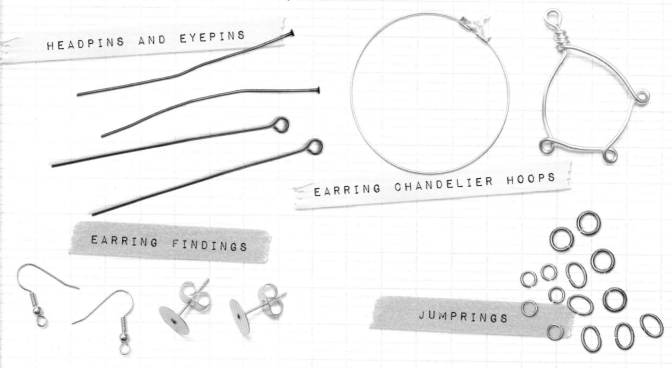

HEADPINS AND EYEPINS

EARRING CHANDELIER HOOPS

EARRING FINDINGS

JUMPRINGS

CRIMP TUBES

This is a little metal tube that you squash using crimping pliers (see page 24) onto a stringing material that can't be knotted, such as nylon-coated steel.

CLASPS

There are so many different types of clasp available to use on your bracelets and necklaces that you will be spoilt for choice. Common styles include the lobster, magnetic, and toggle clasp.

HAIR COMBS AND HAIR BANDS

Available in metal or plastic, combs and bands are a simple hair accessory that you can wrap wire and beads directly onto.

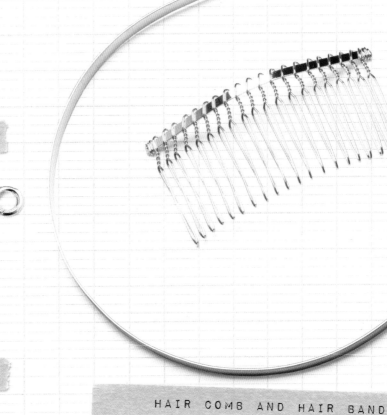

CLASPS

CRIMP TUBES

HAIR COMB AND HAIR BAND

Materials

BROOCH AND KILT PINS

Most brooch backs consist of a hinged pin attached to a long metal bar. This bar has holes in it so you can glue or sew your project onto it. Kilt pins have loops at the bottom that you can hang beads and charms from.

WIRE CHOKERS

A choker is a rigid, thick piece of wire that you can thread or wire beads onto directly.

BANGLE BLANKS

This is a ready-made hinged bangle with a large flat surface on the top, which you can glue your project directly onto. Scuffing the surface with some sandpaper can help the glue adhere to it.

CUFFLINK BLANKS

These come in a variety of sizes and simple shapes and are often flat at the top to allow you to glue your project directly onto them. Alternatively they come with a shallow tray on the top, which is ideal for using resin to embed an object or image (see Skye, page 104).

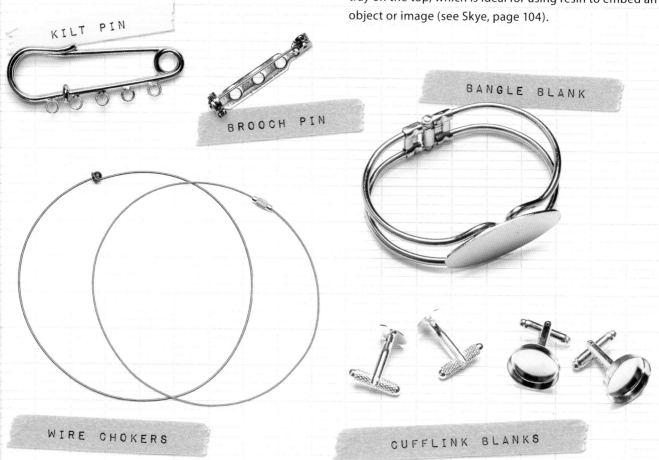

KILT PIN

BROOCH PIN

BANGLE BLANK

WIRE CHOKERS

CUFFLINK BLANKS

Other essentials

You'll need these materials for some of the projects in this book. Experimenting with how you use them will really help you to put your own stamp on things.

RESIN

Resin is a clear liquid plastic. You mix it with a catalyst and it will set rock hard while retaining its crystal clear quality. It is an ideal material for embedding other objects into.

MODELING POLYMER CLAY

This is a clay that once its shaped, can be baked in a household oven and it will become hard and durable. It comes in an enormous variety of colors, so your ideas and shapes have endless possibilities. Try making your own beads with it.

OIL-BASED MODELING CLAY

Soft, pliable oil-based modeling clay (Plastilina or Plasticine) that doesn't harden is handy for using as a prop to push objects into to hold them steady while you work on them.

SHRINK PLASTIC

This is a thin sheet of plastic that you can draw on or stamp with permanent inks, cut out with scissors, and then place in a household oven to bake. It will shrink to a third of its original size, thicken, and become more rigid.

SELF-COVER BUTTONS

Mainly used for upholstery, these buttons can also be highly versatile as jewelry components. They come in many different sizes and you can easily cover them in patterned fabrics to enhance your designs.

OIL-BASED MODELING CLAY

RESIN

SHRINK PLASTIC

SELF-COVER BUTTONS

MODELING POLYMER CLAY

Materials

Techniques

WITH THESE BASIC TECHNIQUES UNDER YOUR BELT YOU WILL BE ABLE TO COMPLETE ALL THE PROJECTS IN THIS BOOK. KEEP PRACTICING AND FOLLOWING THE STEP-BY-STEP PHOTOGRAPHS AND YOU WILL SOON BE ABLE TO MAKE YOUR OWN DESIGNS TOO.

CRIMPING

Give your work a truly professional finish by using crimp tubes and crimping pliers when joining stringing materials to findings. It's a great technique to use when knotting isn't an option.

USING CRIMPING PLIERS

1 Thread a crimp tube onto your stringing material, then pass the thread through the finding and back through the crimp tube. Slide the tube along so that it is close to the finding.

2 Hold the crimp tube in the crescent-shaped section of the crimping pliers and squash the crimp tube into a curved shape, trapping the stringing material.

3 Finish the crimping process by moving the now curved crimp tube to the front circular section of the pliers. Close the pliers tightly, folding the crimp in half.

JUMPRINGS

A neat way for joining your pieces together, jumprings come ready-made in a variety of thicknesses, sizes, shapes, and colored metals—but why not go that extra step and learn to make your own too?

OPENING AND CLOSING JUMPRINGS

1 Hold a jumpring between two pairs of pliers, each with a flat, parallel nose, so that the opening of the jumpring is at the top.

2 Twist the pliers in your left hand away from your body and the pliers in your right hand toward your body. This will open the jumpring without losing the shape of the circle. Twist back the other way to close. Ensure that both the metal edges of the ring click together as you close them.

MAKING JUMPRINGS

1 Coil a length of round wire tightly around a wire-wrap mandrel or multi-sized looping pliers. If you do not have either of these tools, wrap the wire around any cylinder-shaped object (the same size as the jumpring required). The number of coils made will determine the number of jumprings you will make.

2 Slide the coil of wire up until one loop of wire comes off the tool or cylindrical object and—using a piercing saw to create a straight edge—cut through the first coil. Repeat the process, cutting off one ring at a time.

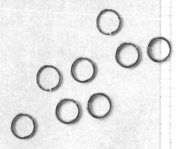

3 Alternatively, use side or top cutters to cut the rings off one at a time.

EYE LOOPS

Eye loops are small loops that are made using round-nose pliers with wire to enable other findings, beads and charms to be attached. You can make the loops permanently closed or possible to be opened again.

CLOSED OR WRAPPED EYE LOOPS

1 Thread a headpin through your chosen bead and then bend the long length of the headpin back against the bead.

2 Using round-nose pliers, grip the wire at the very top of the bead. Then holding the long end of the wire in the other hand, wrap it around the nose of the pliers until it nearly meets itself. It will form a hook shape.

3 Thread this hook shape through some chain or other component that you wish to secure your bead onto.

4 Hold the top of the hook in snipe-nose pliers and the long end of the remaining wire in your other hand. Wrap this long end around the base of the hook, spiraling the wire around itself. Cut off any excess wire. Your bead is now held fast and the only way to remove it is to cut it off!

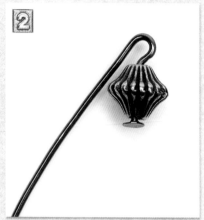

OPEN EYE LOOPS AT THE TOP OF A BEAD

1. Thread a headpin through your chosen bead and then bend the long length of the headpin back against the bead.

2. Using round-nose pliers, grip the wire at the very top of the bead. Then holding the long end of the wire in the other hand, wrap this all the way around the nose of the pliers until the two ends of wire cross each other.

3. Using side or top cutters, cut the excess wire from the long end away at the point where the two wires crossed. You may need to place the loop back in the jaws of your round-nose pliers to form a perfectly circular eye loop.

EYEPINS

An eyepin is a wire with a loop at the end that lets you join other findings to it.

MAKING EYEPINS

1. Using round-nose pliers, hold a piece of wire at the very end. The length of wire you use is determined by the size and number of beads you want to thread onto it, while the size of the eyehole is determined by how far up the nose of the pliers you grip the wire.

2. Twist the pliers to form a small, closed loop.

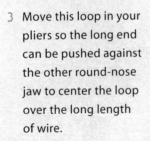

3. Move this loop in your pliers so the long end can be pushed against the other round-nose jaw to center the loop over the long length of wire.

RESIN

Resin is a liquid plastic that usually comes in two parts: the resin itself and a hardener (sometimes called an accelerator or catalyst). Follow the manufacturer's instructions to get the best results with your chosen brand, but here are my top tips for using most types of resin.

WORKING WITH RESIN

1 Make sure your work area is well ventilated, dry and damp free. Cover the work surface in newspaper and ideally wear plastic gloves and goggles when mixing.

2 Get your mold ready before you start mixing. Molds must be clean and free from dust or grease. If need be, prop your mold upright using soft, oil-based modeling clay.

3 Have at least three disposable cups and mixing sticks handy for measuring and mixing your resin. Most types of resin stipulate 50% resin to 50% hardener. In this case, pour the right amount of resin for the project into the first cup. Mark a line on the outside where the resin rests. Then pour into the second cup.

4 Pour your hardener into the first cup up to the drawn line on the outside. Then add this to the measured resin in the second cup. Mix thoroughly with a disposable stick. The third cup is useful if you are adding color to your resin. If resin has different mixing ratios you can draw measurements onto the side of your first cup as a guide.

5 When thoroughly mixed, your resin will contain lots of air bubbles that will eventually disappear during the curing process. Pour your resin into the mold so that it slightly overfills—using its surface tension to keep it from spilling—and leave for at least 24 hours.

POM-POMS

Pom-poms are fun and easy to make. While they are usually made from knitting wool, as in this example, try experimenting with ribbons or strips of fabric for different effects (see Leo, page 68).

MAKING A POM-POM

1 Cut two circles out of stiff card. The size of your circles dictates the size of your finished pom-pom. Then cut out a smaller circle from the middle of each one to form two cardboard rings.

2 Place these two rings on top of each other and start to wrap as long a length of wool as manageable around them. When you have used up that length, simply continue wrapping using another length. You keep repeating this step until you have a very thick "donut" of wool wrapped around both rings.

3 Using sharp fine-pointed scissors or a craft knife, cut through the wool on the outside edge to find the space between the two cardboard rings. When you cut through to the space, it becomes much easier to continue cutting through all the wool. Work your way around the entire edge of the ring.

4 Take another length of wool and place it between the two exposed cardboard rings. Tie a knot as tightly as possible, trapping all the cut pieces of wool.

5 Slide each cardboard ring away and tease the wool into a ball shape. You can trim a few woolen ends if you require a perfect sphere or an alternative shape.

earrings

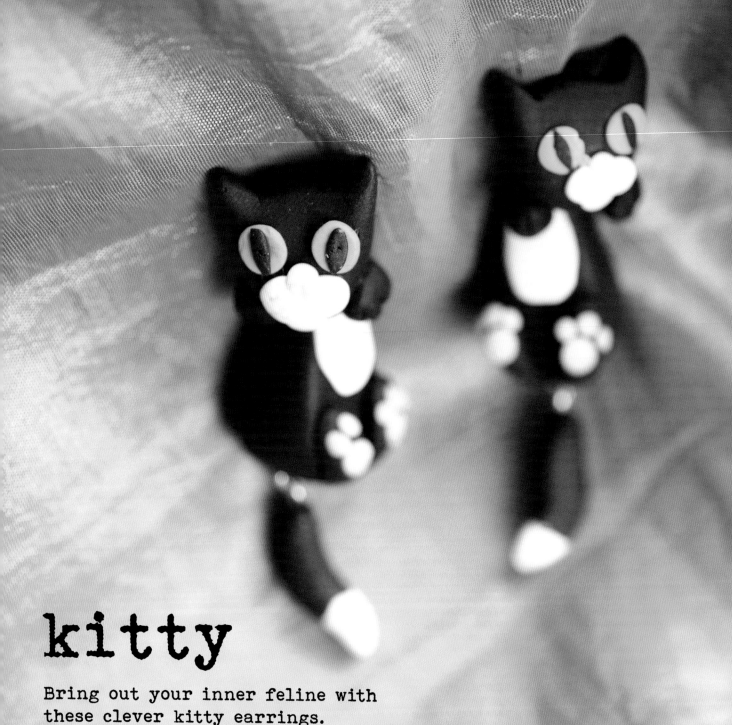

kitty

Bring out your inner feline with these clever kitty earrings.

Everything you will need...

Whether it's a tabby or a ginger tom—with modeling clay coming in an abundance of colors—you can make any cat-lover's favorite variety of kitty!

1 2 x flat-back stud fittings with butterflies

2 6 x ⅝in (15mm) eyepins

3 Black, white, green, and pink modeling clay

Two-part adhesive

Snipe-nose pliers

Flat-nose pliers

Cocktail stick

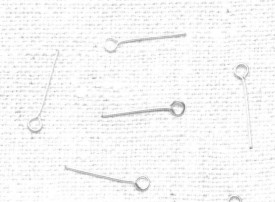

kitty

Assembling kitty

1 Break off a small amount of black clay approximately ³/₄in (18mm) square and mold into a pear shape. Flatten one side by lightly pressing onto a flat surface.

2 Using a small piece of black clay, roll out a sausage shape approximately ³/₁₆in (4mm) in diameter and cut into two equal lengths each about ³/₈in (10mm) long. Place onto the flattened surface at the bottom. Insert an eyepin into the base of the body shape.

3 Take a small amount of white clay and roll out a thin oval shape. Place onto the flattened surface. Then make eight tiny balls of pink clay and press them so they flatten onto the top section of the legs to form paw pads. Insert another eyepin into the top of the body shape.

4 Using black clay, roll out a thick sausage shape and then add a small amount of white clay to one end. Continue rolling so the two clays merge together into a shape approximately ¼in (6mm) thick. Shape the white clay so it forms a tip and insert an eyepin into the other end.

5 Break off another piece of clay, this time around ³/₈in (10mm) square and mold into the shape of a cat's head. Make sure the back of the head is as flat as possible. Roll two small black balls and place onto the bottom of the head.

6 Now you can add the cat's features. Make three small balls using the white clay for the cheeks and one small pink ball for the nose. Again, when you add these they will flatten. Roll out the green clay and cut out two small circles. Add tiny strips of black clay to each one to make the pupils. Place these onto the head. Using a cocktail stick you can add some dots to the white cheeks for extra effect. Bake all the pieces in the oven following the instructions on the packets of clay.

7 When cool, open the end of the eye loop on the tail and link it to the bottom eye loop on the cat's body and close.

8 Open the eye loop at the top of the cat's body and link onto the loop of a stud butterfly.

9 Glue the flat-back stud fitting onto the flat surface at the back of the cat's head using two-part adhesive and leave to dry. Repeat all the steps to make the other earring.

YOU CAN KEEP THE EYEPINS IN THE CLAY WHILE IT BAKES BUT ONCE THEY HAVE COOLED YOU MAY NEED TO ADD A DROP OF GLUE IF THEY FEEL LOOSE.

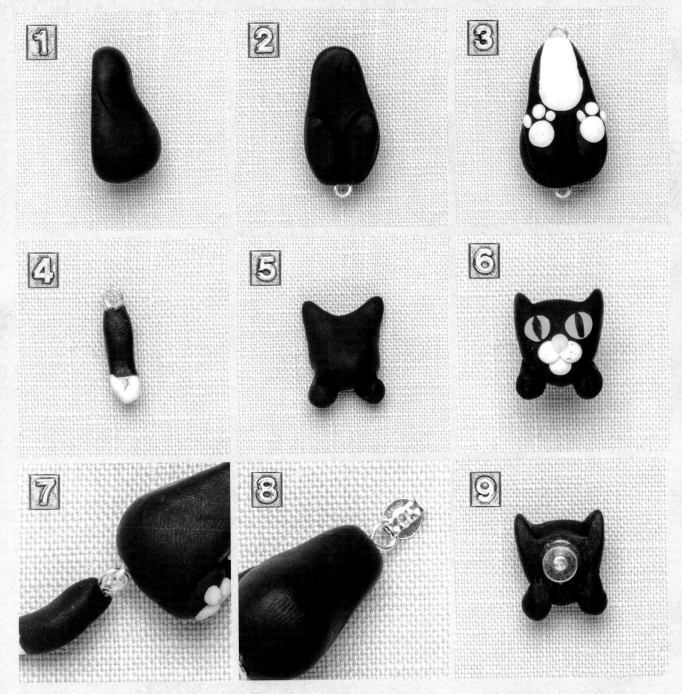

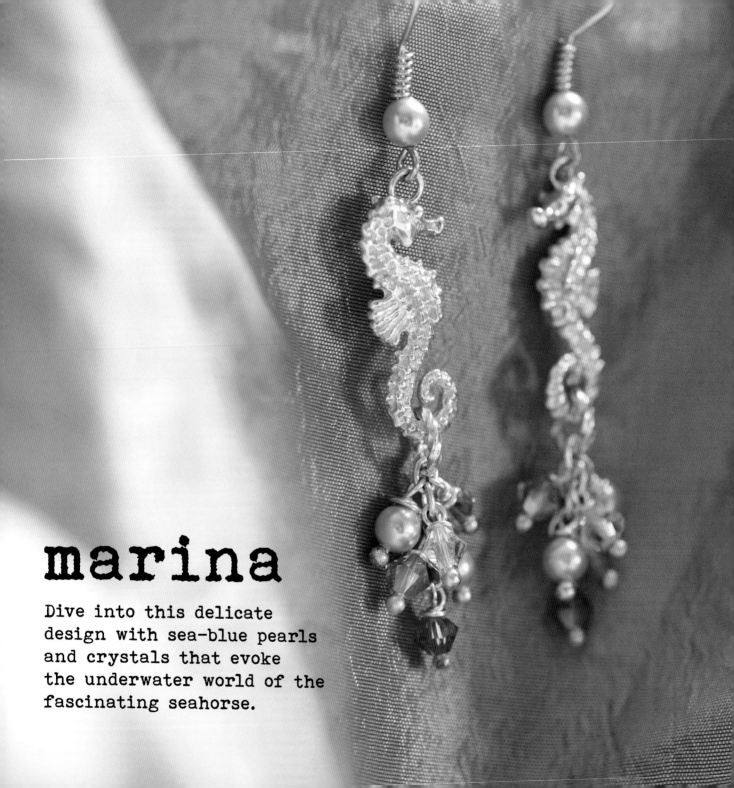

marina

Dive into this delicate
design with sea-blue pearls
and crystals that evoke
the underwater world of the
fascinating seahorse.

Everything you will need...

It's all in the detail—replacing the silver ball on an earring hook with a blue pearl adds a special touch to this design.

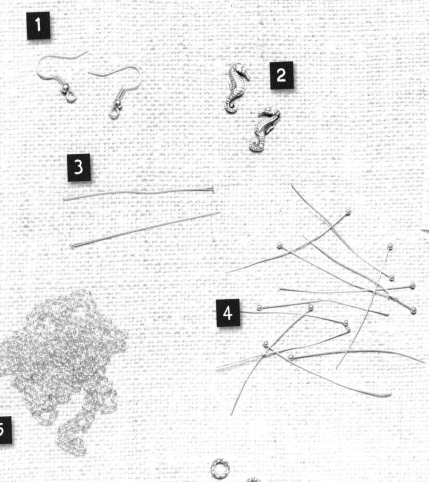

1 2 x silver earring hook wires

2 2 x silver seahorse charms

3 2 x 2in (50mm) flat headpins

4 12 x 2in (50mm) ball headpins

5 1³/₁₆in (30mm) small link silver trace chain

6 2 x 6mm twisted silver jumprings

7 14 x 4mm assorted blue crystals and pearls

Round-nose pliers

Flat-nose pliers

Snipe-nose pliers

Side cutters

marina

Assembling marina

1 Thread one flat headpin through one of the seahorse charms and make an open eye loop as close as possible to the top of the seahorse's head.

2 Open one twisted jumpring and loop it onto the tail of the seahorse and then link on five links of the small trace chain and close.

3 Take one ball headpin and thread through the darkest colored crystal from your assortment of beads. Using round-nose pliers, make a hook shape as close to the top of the bead as possible.

4 Thread the wire of the hook through the last link of chain hanging from your seahorse's tail. Hold the hook in a pair of snipe pliers. Holding the long end of wire in your fingers, wrap it around the base of the hook to form a closed eye loop—securing the bead onto the chain. Cut away any excess wire.

5 Thread two ball headpins through two assorted beads and make hooks on them both as you did in step 3. Then hook one bead onto the left-hand side of the first link of chain hanging directly from the twisted jumpring on the seahorse's tail. Then, as before, wrap the long end of wire around the base of the hook to form a closed eye loop. Repeat this step, threading the other bead directly to the right on the same link.

6 Thread another two beads in the same way but this time thread them to the left and right of the third link down on the trace chain.

7 Thread one ball headpin through another bead and again form a hook as close to the top of the bead as possible. This time thread the hook through the second link down on the chain so it falls between the four beads you have already added. Again, wrap the wire to form a closed loop and then cut away any excess wire.

8 Take your silver earring hook wire and open the loop at the bottom so the wire is straightened out. Remove the silver ball and replace it with one blue bead. Reform the eye loop at the bottom of the earring hook using round-nose pliers. Don't completely close the loop.

9 Take your seahorse charm and thread it onto the open loop on the earring hook you made in step 8. Completely close the loop on the earring hook. Repeat all the steps to make the other earring.

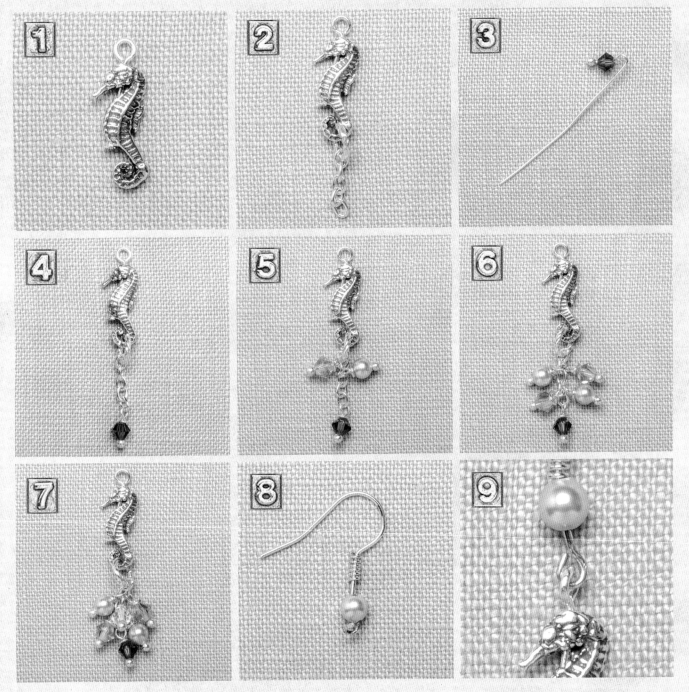

chichi

One of the rarest animals in the world but also one of the
cutest, pandas take center stage on these striking earrings.

Everything you will need...

With their bold black-and-white markings pandas make an iconic motif for any design. The only difficulty is deciding which print to choose from the hundreds available.

1 2 x $^{15}/_{16}$in (24mm) white, plastic self-cover buttons

2 Panda-print fabric

3 2 x $^{5}/_{16}$in (8mm) flat-back earring studs with butterflies

Two-part adhesive

Scissors

Craft knife

Needle

Green thread

Assembling chichi

1 Draw a circle approximately $^3/_8$in (10mm) larger than your panda face on your printed fabric.

2 Cut out the circle with a pair of scissors.

3 Using cotton and a dressmaking needle, sew a running thread loosely around the edge of the circle leaving the ends long.

4 Place the fabric over the white, plastic dome of the self-cover button and pull the two loose ends of cotton so it gathers tightly around the button. Check that you're happy with where the panda face is positioned and then tie the cotton ends together. Cut any excess thread.

5 Take the flat disc section of the self-cover button and snap it onto the back of the dome. It will click and lock into place. Use a sharp craft knife to cut away the excess peg from the back.

6 Mix a small quantity of two-part adhesive and glue the flat-back stud fitting onto the back of the button at the top. Repeat all the steps to make the other earring.

SELF-COVER BUTTONS COME IN A VARIETY OF SIZES SO YOU CAN MAKE LARGE OR SMALL STUD EARRINGS.

DOUBLE-CHECK THE POSITION OF YOUR FLAT-BACK STUD
FITTING BEFORE GLUING IT TO ENSURE YOUR PANDA'S
FACE IS THE RIGHT WAY UP.

spike

These creepy-crawly caterpillars will turn heads as they wriggle on your earrings.

Everything you will need...

Using wire to thread on the beads means you can shape your caterpillars' bodies to make them as wriggly as you like.

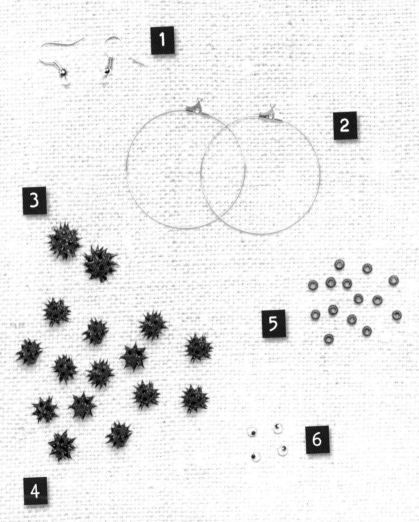

1. 2 x silver earring hooks
2. 2 x 2in (50mm) silver earring hoop chandeliers
3. 2 x 8mm spiky rubber beads
4. 14 x 6mm spiky rubber beads
5. 14 x 4mm pink wooden seed beads
6. 4 x ⅛in (3mm) eyes
7. 2 x 8in (200mm) lengths of US 22-gauge (SWG 23, 0.6mm) pink wire

Superglue

Side cutters

Round-nose pliers

Flat-nose pliers

Snipe-nose pliers

Assembling spike

1 Cut 2in (50mm) of the pink wire and—holding the very end in a pair of round-nose pliers—form a small spiral. Repeat this step on the end of the remaining 6in (150mm) length of the wire.

2 Thread both pieces of wire through one of the 8mm spiky rubber beads and then through one of the wooden beads. Holding the two spirals so they don't move, start to wrap the smaller piece of wire around the longer length to secure it in place.

3 Cut the excess wire off the small length and then continue to alternately thread onto the remaining long length of wire one 6mm spiky rubber bead and one wooden bead until you have threaded on seven of the smaller rubber beads.

4 Holding all the rubber beads on the length of wire as snugly together as possible, start to wrap the remaining exposed length of wire around the silver earring hoop chandelier several times. Cut off any excess wire.

5 Form the caterpillar body inside the hoop chandelier so it looks like it is moving. You may need to add a drop of glue where the spiky beads touch the hoop to keep it in place.

6 Trim some spikes off the 8mm spiky rubber bead. Add two drops of glue and stick on two eyes. Spread the spiraled wires apart to look like antennae.

7 Open the loop at the bottom of a silver earring hook, link it onto the loop on the silver hoop chandelier, and close. Repeat all the steps for the other earring.

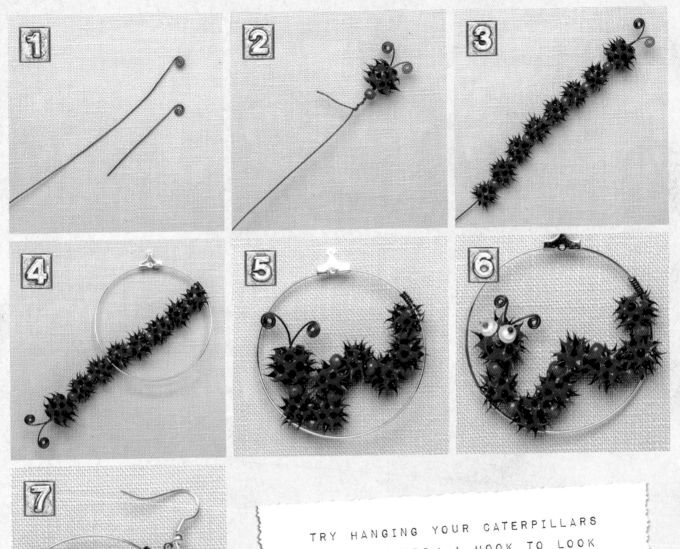

TRY HANGING YOUR CATERPILLARS DIRECTLY FROM A HOOK TO LOOK LIKE THEY HAVE JUST CRAWLED OUT OF YOUR EAR!

spike

bracelets

fenton

"Man's best friend" will make you everyone's
best friend as they'll all want one of these
fabulous dog charm bracelets on their wrist.

Everything you will need...

You can put anyone under your spell by making them a charm bracelet using these simple techniques. Charms come in such an enormous variety of styles and colors that you're sure to find something to appeal.

1. 1 x silver collar and bone toggle clasp
2. 1 x 6in (150mm) length of silver curb chain
3. 10 x 4mm silver jumprings
4. 8 x assorted silver dog charms

Flat-nose pliers

Snipe-nose pliers

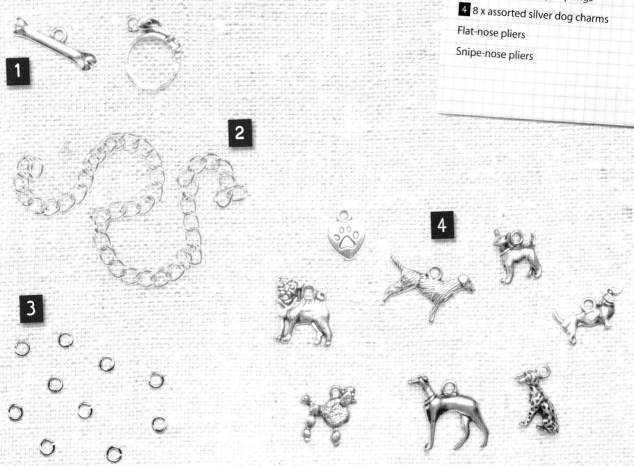

Assembling fenton

1 Open a jumpring and thread on the bone toggle, then join it onto the end link of the curb chain and close.

2 Open another jumpring and thread on the collar clasp. Join it onto the end link at the other end of the curb chain and close.

3 Open the next jumpring and thread on a charm and then link onto the large loop on the collar clasp and close.

4 Lay the bracelet out flat and place the remaining seven charms along the length, planning where you are going to link them.

5 Open a jumpring and thread on your first dog charm. Join it onto the planned link on the chain and close.

6 Open another jumpring and thread on the next dog charm and join it onto the next planned link on the chain and close. Keep your chain links from twisting so that your charms hang in the same direction and repeat this step until all the charms are added.

THE SIZE OF AN AVERAGE ADULT WRIST IS 6-8$\frac{1}{2}$IN (15-22CM) INCLUDING THE CLASP. A CHILD'S WRIST IS 4-6IN (10-15CM). ALWAYS MEASURE YOUR WRIST TO OBTAIN THE CORRECT CHAIN LENGTH.

Animals

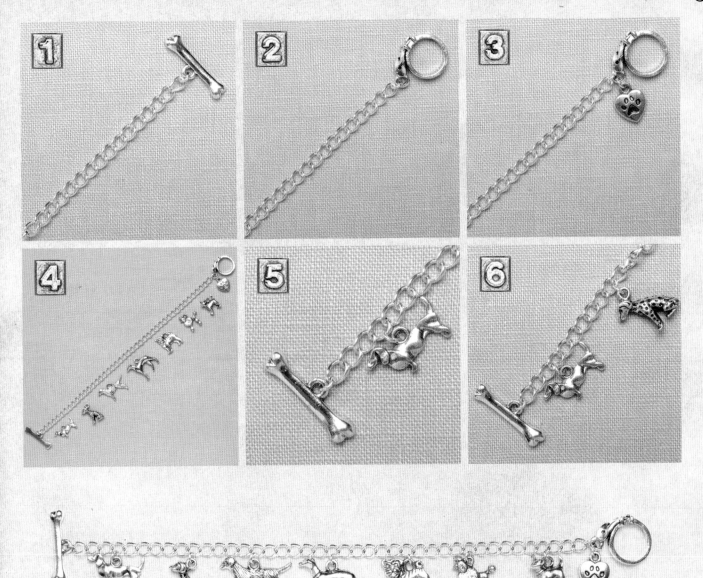

USING A DECORATIVE TOGGLE CLASP, LIKE THIS COLLAR AND BONE,
REALLY ENHANCES THE THEME OF THE DESIGN.

fenton

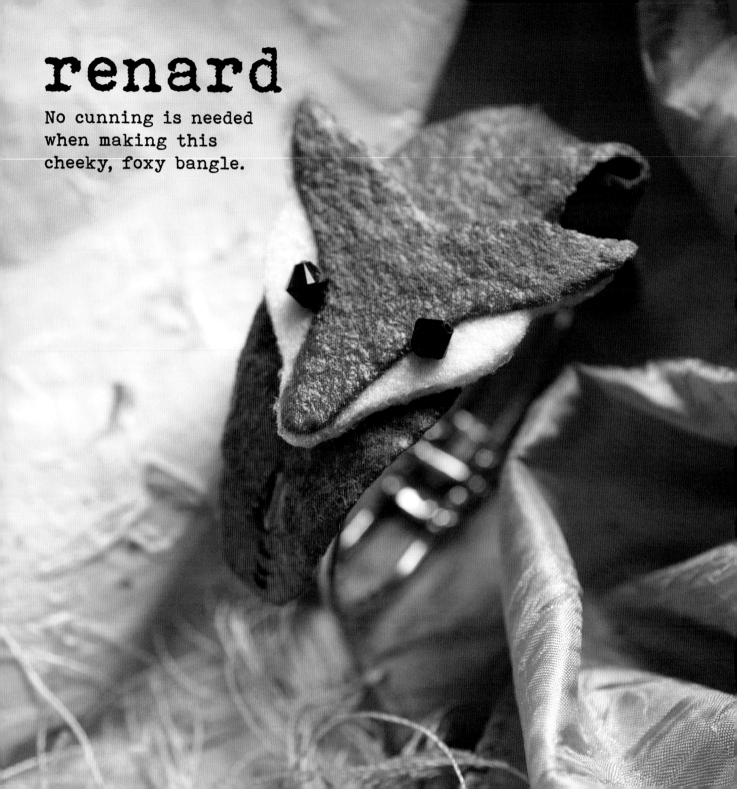

renard

No cunning is needed
when making this
cheeky, foxy bangle.

Everything you will need...

Create curves in felt by using white (PVA) glue. It is a marvelous setting agent for fabrics, allowing you to create natural, organic shapes.

1 1 x bangle blank

2 2 x 6mm black bicone crystal beads

3 1 x square of thick white felt

4 1 x square of thick orange felt

White (PVA) glue

Two-part adhesive

Scissors

Pencil

Paintbrush

Needle and black cotton

Plastic wrap (cling film)

Tape

1

2

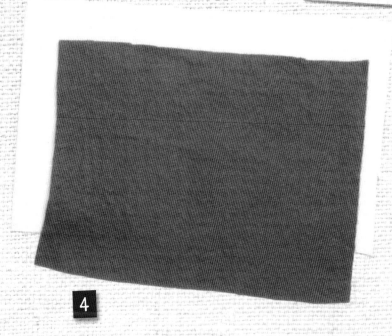

3

4

renard

5656

Assembling renard

1 Draw the shapes for the fox's body, nose, and ears onto the orange felt (see templates on page 120). On the white felt draw the tip of a tail and the shape of the fox's face. Cut out all of the shapes with a pair of scissors.

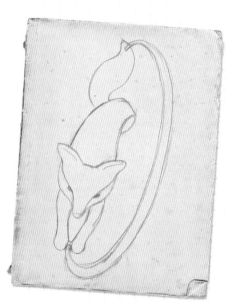

2 Pour some white (PVA) glue into a pot and place all of your felt shapes into it. Ensure that all the surfaces are covered in glue. Place a piece of plastic wrap over a cylindrical shape that is slightly bigger than your wrist; a mug is a good size. Take the felt body and twist it into an organic shape and place over the plastic wrap-covered former. Stick the white tail tip on.

3 Place the white felt face onto a flat plastic wrap-covered surface and lay the orange felt nose shape onto it. Leave them all to completely dry. Drying time can be up to 24 hours. The felt should be rigid enough to hold its shape. If it still feels floppy, paint on another layer of white glue and again leave to dry. Sew the bicone black crystals onto the face shape. Try to mirror the crystals so the beads are facing up and away to look like eyes.

4 You can also sew on some details like claws on the fox's paws. If you have good sewing skills, why not try to embroider some flowers onto the body for a quirky detail?

5 Mix a small quantity of two-part adhesive and cover the blank surface on the top of the bangle. Stick the stiff felt body shape onto the blank and hold it in place with some tape while the glue hardens.

6 Finally, mix another small quantity of the two-part adhesive and cover a small area on the top of the felt body. Put the head in place and press firmly to secure it before leaving to dry.

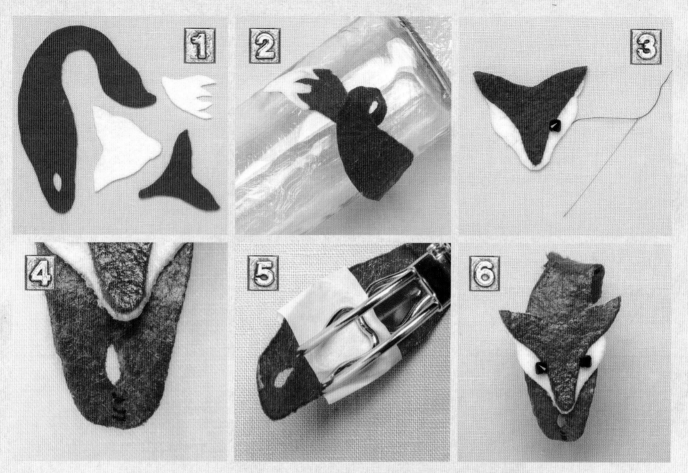

WHEN DRAWING ONTO THE FELT,
ENSURE YOU USE A PENCIL AND NOT A
FELT-TIP PEN OR MARKER AS THESE WILL
RUN WHEN WET AND STAIN YOUR FELT.

renard

kaa

The hypnotic spiral eyes on this slithery bangle
are based on my childhood memories of Kaa the
snake from the classic *The Jungle Book*.

Everything you will need...

Keep your beads on the small side so the memory wire doesn't get overloaded, as it may distort.

1. Roll of bangle-size memory wire
2. Roll of US 28-gauge (SWG 30, 0.3mm) black beading wire
3. 1³/₁₆in (20mm) red suede ribbon
4. 26 x snake-print beads

Heavy-duty pliers with cutter or memory-wire cutters

Round-nose pliers

Side cutters

Scissors

Craft knife

Superglue

4 x26

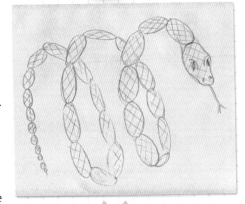

Assembling kaa

1 Cut your roll of bangle-sized memory wire using your cutters. Ensure you have at least four coils in your length of wire.

2 Thread one of the snake-print beads onto the coil and—using round-nose pliers—make an eye loop at the end of the wire. Bend the loop so that it catches under the bead.

3 Cut 2³/₄in (70mm) from the coil of beading wire and using the tip of your round-nose pliers, make a tiny spiral at either end. Continue to spiral the wire around itself at each end until you are left with 1³/₁₆in (20mm) of straight wire remaining between them. Then bend the wire at the middle point between both spirals to form a "V" shape.

4 Bend this "V" shape around the end of the bead, making sure that the bottom of the "V" catches under the eye loop you added in step 2. Add a drop of superglue to the beading wire to hold it in place.

5 Cut 1³/₁₆in (20mm) of red suede ribbon and—using a craft knife—cut a "V" shape out of the end. You will also need to taper the other end so that it is thin enough to fit through the hole of your snake bead. Add a drop of superglue to the tapered end.

6 When the superglue has dried on the red suede it will have gone very hard. This makes it a lot easier to push through the hole of the bead. Add another drop of superglue to the hole and then push the tapered end into it and leave to dry.

7 Add all the remaining snake beads to the memory wire, ensuring you keep them all pushed snugly next to each other.

8 When all the beads are added, hold the memory wire in the jaws of your round-nose pliers and make an eye loop as close to the last bead as possible, to secure them all in place. Cut away the excess memory wire again, using old or specially made cutters (see tip).

CUTTING MEMORY WIRE WILL BLUNT JEWELRY CUTTERS VERY QUICKLY SO IT'S BEST TO USE AN OLD PAIR OR CUTTERS DESIGNED ESPECIALLY FOR THE JOB.

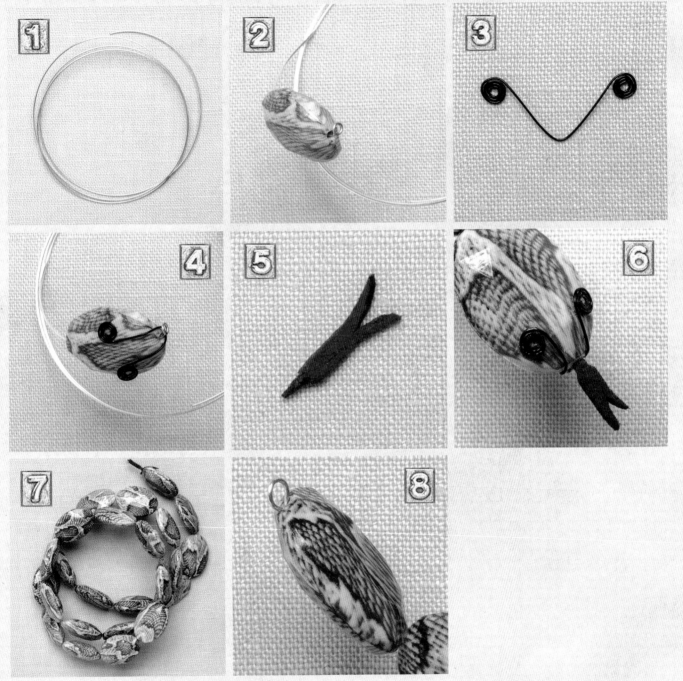

tembo

You'll want to blow your own trumpet when you've made this
beautiful bracelet inspired by the majestic African elephant!

Everything you will need...

Using assorted carved wooden beads in multiple rows gives this bracelet a real African vibe.

1. 4 x 40mm wooden separators
2. 8 x 14mm elephant beads
3. 4 x 10mm brown feature beads
4. 24 x assorted black-and-white carved wooden beads
5. Roll of beading elastic

Ruler

Scissors

Bead mat

tembo

Assembling tembo

1 To make a bracelet to comfortably fit an average adult's wrist you will need to have enough beads to line up over 7¹/₂in (190mm). Start by laying your beads out along a ruler's edge, so you can obtain an even pattern as well as knowing how many beads you will need to reach the required length. I have used 12 assorted beads for each length of elastic.

2 Cut three 15in (380mm) lengths of beading elastic from the roll. It's good to cut the lengths a little longer than required because it makes them easier to tie together at the end.

3 Take your first piece of elastic and thread your beads directly onto it in the same formation as you planned in step 1.

4 Thread your remaining pieces of elastic in the same way. When they are all threaded, check that now they are all beaded they are still all the same length.

5 When all the beads are threaded on, simply tie the corresponding ends together in a double knot and cut off the excess elastic ³/₁₆in (5mm) away from the knot. Move the elastic around so the knot is hidden inside a bead.

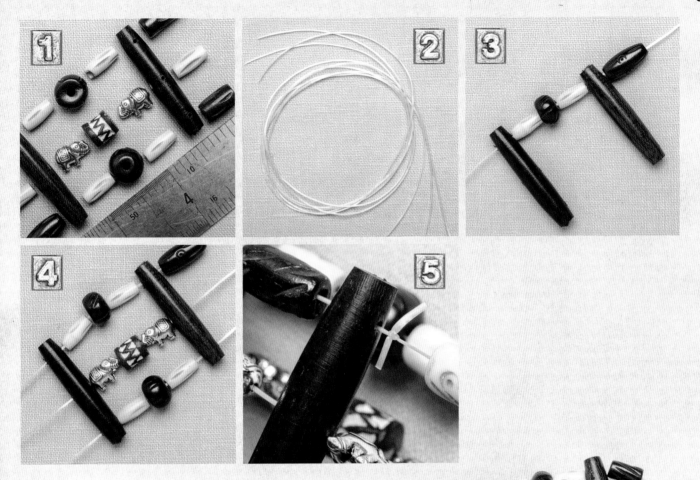

CUT EXCESS ELASTIC SLIGHTLY AWAY FROM
THE KNOT SO IT WON'T UNRAVEL THROUGH
WEAR. FOR EXTRA SECURITY YOU CAN ADD
A DROP OF SUPERGLUE.

necklaces

leo

This bold and tactile statement choker
is bound to be a **roaring** success!

Everything you will need...

Using two-tone organza creates a fabulous color effect. You could also try the more traditional method of using wool to make your lion's mane.

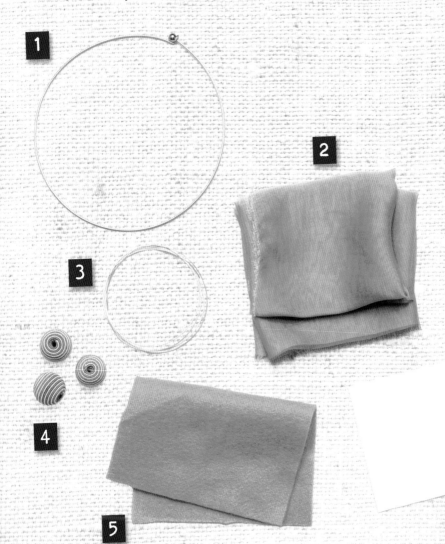

1. 1 x 16in (405mm) of gold choker wire
2. 20 x 20in (500 x 500mm) of two-tone organza
3. 6in (150mm) of US 20-gauge (SWG 21, 0.8mm) gold wire
4. 3 x 22mm cord beads
5. 1 x sheet of tan-colored felt
6. 1 x sheet of stiff cardboard

Side cutters

Snipe-nose pliers

Needle

Tan-colored cotton thread

Scissors

Craft knife

Latex-based rubber cement (Copydex)

Felt-tip pens

Assembling leo

1 Cut a small slit approximately ¹³/₁₆in (20mm) from the edge of your fabric and tear the strip off with your hands. This will give you a perfect straight edge of organza, as it is tearing along the weave. Then holding the edges of the fabric, pull some of the threads away to leave a fluffy edge. Keep repeating this step so you have 15 strips of fabric all the same length.

2 Cut two circles with a diameter of 2in (50mm) from your sheet of stiff card. Then cut a 1³/₁₆in (30mm) hole out of the center of each circle to leave a ³/₈in (10mm) ring. Place these two rings on top of each other and start to wrap the strips of fabric around the rings. When you finish wrapping one strip, just start another one on top. There's no need to tie them together.

3 When you have used all 15 strips, slide a craft knife through the strips of fabric to find the space between the cardboard rings. Once located, continue slicing the fabric strips—or alternatively swap to scissors—and carry on cutting all the way around the ring edge.

4 Cut another strip of organza and place it between the two cardboard rings that are now fully exposed and tie a knot as tightly as possible. This will trap all the cut pieces of organza and you will be able to slide each cardboard ring away, leaving you with a fluffy pom-pom. Do not cut away the long ends from the knot yet.

5 Draw the shape of the lion's head onto your tan felt and cut it out. Using fine point felt-tip pens, draw on the lion's face.

6 Cut two small triangles from your felt and—using a needle and tan-colored thread—pinch the triangle so it forms an ear shape. Sew a few stitches to hold it in place.

7 Holding the pom-pom with the tie ends at the center back, you should be able to part the organza strips and flatten them down to the strip that is holding everything. Glue the lion's felt face at this point. When it is dry, sew your two ears set slightly back above the face.

8 Hold the pom-pom so the face is at the front and the tie ends are at the back. Part the organza strips at one side to reveal where the central hole of the rings used to be. Thread your 6in (150mm) length of gold wire all the way through at this point. You can now cut away the long ties at the back of the pom-pom.

9 Take your gold choker wire and unscrew the ball at one end. Thread on one of your cord beads. Then, holding your lion's head against the choker, start to wrap one end of the gold wire around it. Cut away the excess wire after several coils. Wrap the other end of the gold wire around the choker several times and cut away the excess wire. Finally, thread on the other two beads and screw the ball back on the choker.

bubbles

There may be plenty of fish in the sea but nothing quite like this shimmering shoal necklace complete with blue bubbles.

Everything you will need...

Fish beads come in an array of shapes and colors so you can make your design really unique.

1. 1 x reel of US 26-gauge (SWG 27, 0.4mm) blue nylon-coated steel wire
2. 1 x 20mm fish clasp
3. 1 x 16mm closed, twisted jumpring
4. 2 x 8mm blue beads
5. 30 x 2mm x 1mm silver crimp tubes
6. 20 x blue, spotty 10mm beads
7. 16 x 2mm (size 10) blue seed beads
8. 14 x fish-shaped beads

Side cutters

Crimping pliers

Flat-nose pliers

Metallic marker pen

Superglue

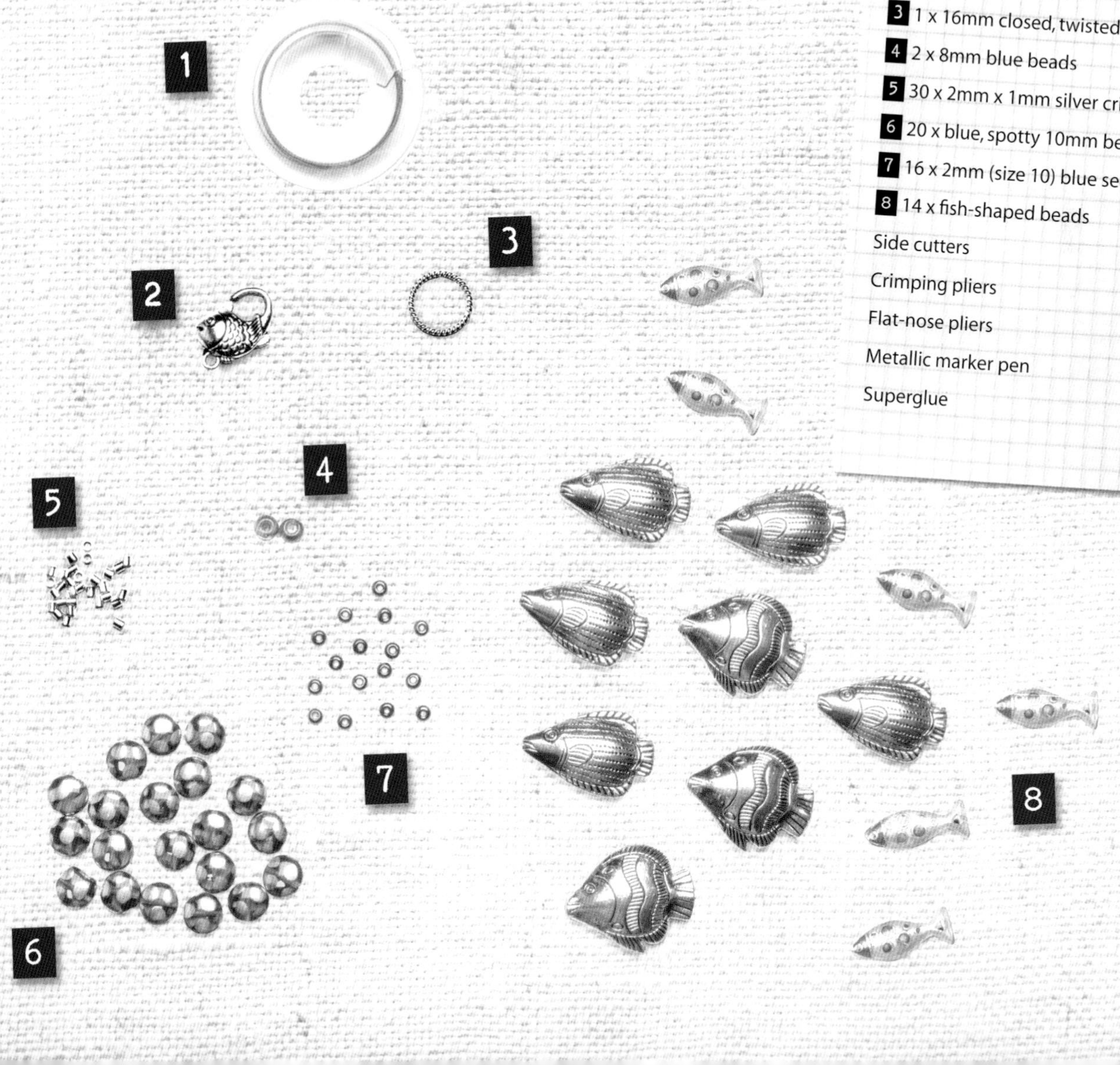

bubbles

Assembling bubbles

1 Cut three lengths of the nylon-coated steel wire each at 20in (50cm) long. Holding all three pieces together, thread them all through a crimp tube, through the loop on the fish clasp, and then back through the crimp tube. Slide the crimp tube so it meets the fish clasp and traps all the wires evenly. Using crimping pliers, crimp the tube into place.

2 Take one of the 8mm blue beads and again thread all three wires through it. Slide the bead up and over the crimped tube to cover it and add a drop of glue to hold it in position. Cut away the excess short wires.

3 Lay your three wires flat so that they are staggered. The top one must be 16in (40cm) in length. Place your beads and fish along the wires so that they are randomly spaced out. Taking a metallic marker pen, mark where each fish is going to be positioned on each wire. Then remove all the beads.

4 Starting with the top wire, add your beads and then before adding your first fish bead, slide a crimp tube onto the wire. Then add the fish bead before sliding on another crimp tube. Using flat-nose pliers, squash the crimp tube flat onto the wire at the first point you marked in metallic pen. Then squash the other crimp tube flat directly behind the fish, securing it in place. Continue adding your beads, crimp tubes, and fish along all the wires, securing them as you go.

5 Holding the three wires together at the open end, thread them through another 8mm blue bead. Then thread them all through a crimp tube, around the closed jumpring, and back through the crimp tube. Slide the crimp tube toward the jumpring, holding all the wires nice and tight. Using crimping pliers, crimp the tube into place.

6 Slide the 8mm bead up and over the crimped tube to cover it and add another drop of glue to hold it in position. Cut away the excess short wires.

7 Lay your necklace out flat again. Move the seed beads and 10mm beads along the wires so that they appear to be floating mid-way along the wires. Add tiny drops of superglue at each one securing them all into place along the wires.

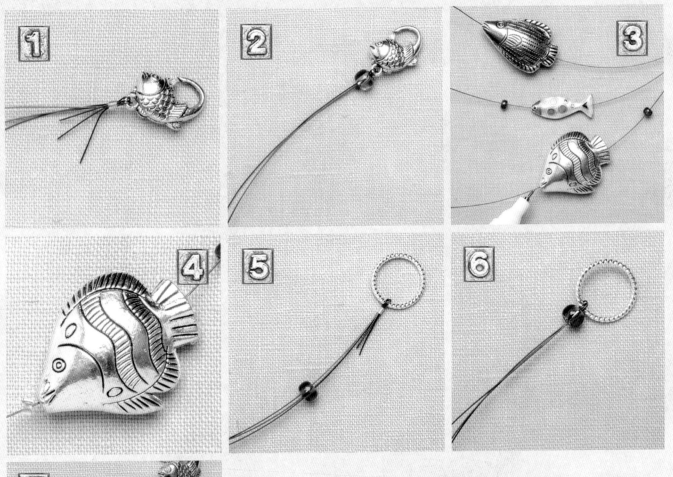

MAKE SURE YOUR FISH BEADS HAVE
HOLES RUNNING FROM HEAD TO TAIL
SO WHEN THEY ARE STRUNG THEY
HANG THE RIGHT WAY.

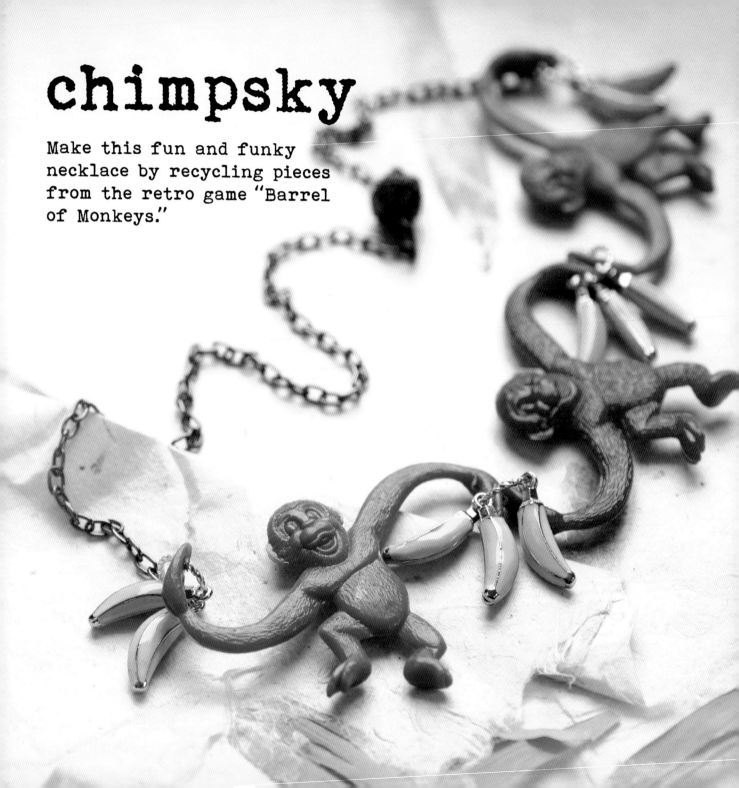

chimpsky

Make this fun and funky necklace by recycling pieces from the retro game "Barrel of Monkeys."

Everything you will need...

Get up to some monkey business by adding these banana charms for a colorful, quirky edge.

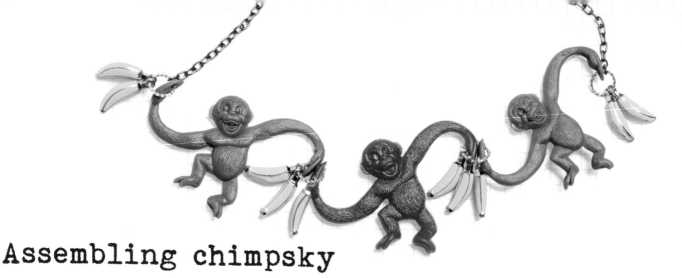

Assembling chimpsky

1 Holding one blue monkey firmly in your hand, use a small $^1/_8$in (2mm) drill bit and twist it slowly through the tip of the monkey's right hand.

2 Take the red monkey and line up its left hand against the hole drilled through the blue monkey. Push the drill bit through the hole you made. Start to twist the drill bit so that it now makes a hole in the red monkey's left hand.

3 Open a 10mm twisted jumpring and thread it through the holes you made in the blue and red monkeys' hands. Add three banana charms and close the jumpring. Use the same method to attach the other blue monkey by his left hand to your red monkey that is already linked.

4 You now have a blue monkey either side of a red one. Starting with the blue monkey on the right, twist the drill bit to make a hole in the monkey's left hand.

5 Take another twisted jumpring and thread it through the hole you have made in the blue monkey's left hand. Link on two banana charms and 8½in (215mm) of red chain and close. Take the last twisted jumpring and thread it through the hole on the left monkey's right hand, add two more banana charms and 4½in (110mm) of red chain and close.

6 Open the two red jumprings and link one each through the loops on either side of a magnetic clasp. Link on each end of the red chain to either jumpring and close.

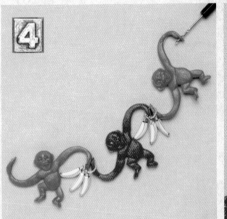

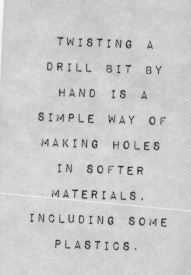

TWISTING A
DRILL BIT BY
HAND IS A
SIMPLE WAY OF
MAKING HOLES
IN SOFTER
MATERIALS.
INCLUDING SOME
PLASTICS.

chimpsky

octavia

This is one spider that won't be giving you a fright!
Make the prettiest eight-legged arachnid to wear
around your neck.

Everything you will need...

A choker is a great option for this necklace, but you could try dangling this spider from a long chain to make it look as though it is crawling up your body.

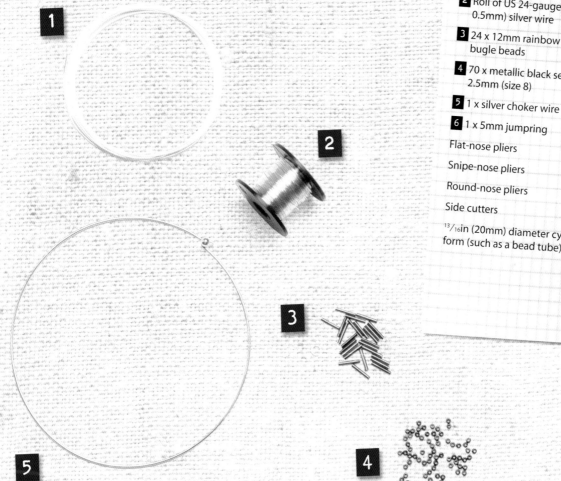

1 11¾in (300mm) of US 18-gauge (SWG 19, 1mm) silver wire

2 Roll of US 24-gauge (SWG 25, 0.5mm) silver wire

3 24 x 12mm rainbow black bugle beads

4 70 x metallic black seed beads 2.5mm (size 8)

5 1 x silver choker wire

6 1 x 5mm jumpring

Flat-nose pliers

Snipe-nose pliers

Round-nose pliers

Side cutters

¹³⁄₁₆in (20mm) diameter cylindrical form (such as a bead tube)

octavia

Assembling octavia

1 Take the 11³/₄in (300mm) length of silver wire and place it centrally over a ¹³/₁₆in (20mm) cylindrical form—so that 6in (150mm) of wire hangs from either side of the form. Wrap the wire around the form so the wires cross over and then slide it off. Then place a smaller cylindrical shape, like a biro pen, at where the wires cross. Wrap them back around the pen, forming a figure of eight shape.

2 Using flat-nose pliers, bend one of the wires straight up at the top of the figure of eight. Then using round-nose pliers, form a small open eye loop ³/₁₆in (4mm) up the length of straight wire. Then take the other long length of wire and wrap it around the straight length of wire, tightly coiling it as you go until it meets the eye loop. Cut away the excess wire.

3 Cut 6in (150mm) from the coil of US 24-gauge (SWG 25, 0.5mm) thin silver wire and make a tiny spiral at one end, using round-nose pliers. Then bend the wire up at 90 degrees to the spiral so that it looks similar to a headpin.

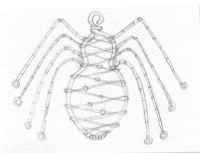

4 Onto this wire thread one bugle bead followed by a seed bead, another bugle bead, then a seed bead, and a final bugle bead. Hold the beads close to where the figure of eight circles cross and start to coil the wire tightly around the middle.

5 Wrap the wire along the join a couple of times until it is close to the edge of the circle, then add another row of beads to match the previous row. When you have threaded on the last bugle bead, cut the excess wire so you only have ³/₈in (10mm) showing. Hold the tip of the wire in your round-nose pliers and start to spiral the wire around itself so it coils toward the last bugle bead added, keeping them all in place.

6 Repeat steps 3–5 to attach three more lengths of the wire to form the spider's eight legs.

7 Cut 11³/₄in (300mm) of US 24-gauge (SWG 25, 0.5mm) thin silver wire from the roll and wrap one end tightly around the top of the larger circle close to where all the legs have been added. Coil it around the thicker US 18-gauge (SWG 19, 1mm) wire shape at least four times. Then add several seed beads to this wire so that when you cross to the other side of the shape, the beads form a tight row. Wrap the thin wire tightly around the thicker wire. Do not cut the wire.

8 Keep adding seed beads to the thin wire and criss-cross inside the circle shape to form a stripy body. When you have created at least four lines, wrap the remaining length of wire around the thick wire shape at the bottom. Cut away any excess thin wire.

9 Cut 4in (100mm) of the thin silver wire and thread three seed beads onto it. Center them on the wire and then bend it in half so it forms a small triangle of beads. Hold this triangle on the head of the spider and wrap both ends of wire around the thicker wire circle shape four times. Repeat this step to add the other eye to the head. Link the spider on to your choker wire using the jumpring.

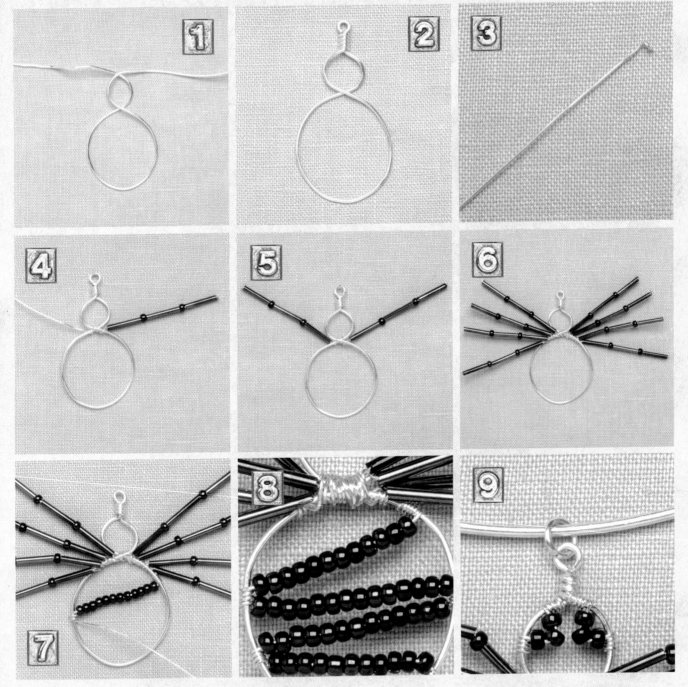

brooches

opo

This fun kilt pin will become
a firm favorite, just like
the playful dolphins
that inspired it.

Everything you will need...

The childlike quality of these enameled bottlenose-dolphin charms gave me the idea to have beads like beach balls alongside for them to play with.

1. 1 x 3in (76mm) silver five-loop kilt pin
2. 3 x dolphin charms
3. 2 x 6mm striped round beads
4. 2 x 2in (50mm) flat headpins
5. Reel of US 21-gauge (SWG 22, 0.7mm) blue wire

Side cutters

Flat-nose pliers

Snipe-nose pliers

Round-nose pliers

Red nail varnish

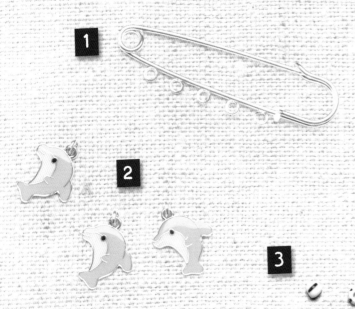

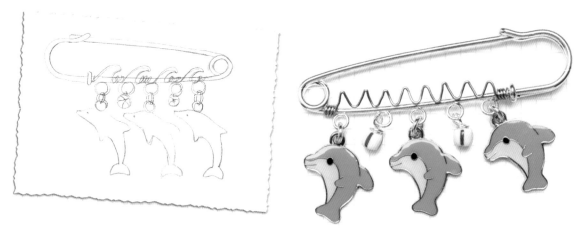

Assembling opo

1 Cut 8in (200mm) of wire from the reel and bend it in half.

2 Slide a pair of flat-nose pliers right up to the fold and then bend the wire back over the jaw of the pliers, creating a zigzag shape as you work along the wire.

3 When you have made eight points, lightly squash each tip into a sharper point using your flat-nose pliers.

4 Stretch the wire out so it forms even points and fits on the kilt pin above the loops.

5 Coil the remaining wire tightly around the kilt pin either side of the end loops and then cut away any excess wire.

6 Open the jumpring at the top of one of your charms and link it through the first left-hand loop on your kilt pin and close. Repeat this step with the other two charms, linking one onto the middle loop and one on the end right loop.

7 Take your flat headpins and, using red nail varnish, paint the end of the pins and leave them to dry.

8 Thread a headpin through one of the stripy beads and form a hook as close to the top of the bead as possible. Thread this hook through the second empty loop along on the kilt pin.

9 Grip the hook in the jaws of your snipe-nose pliers. Wrap the long end of wire on the headpin around the base of the hook, forming a spiral of wire on top of the bead. Cut away any excess wire. Attach the other stripy bead to the remaining empty loop on the kilt pin in the same way.

WHEN PAINTING NAIL VARNISH ONTO A HEADPIN IT IS BEST TO LIGHTLY SAND THE HEAD OF THE PIN WITH A PIECE OF EMERY PAPER FIRST SO THE COLOR ADHERES TO THE METAL.

Animals

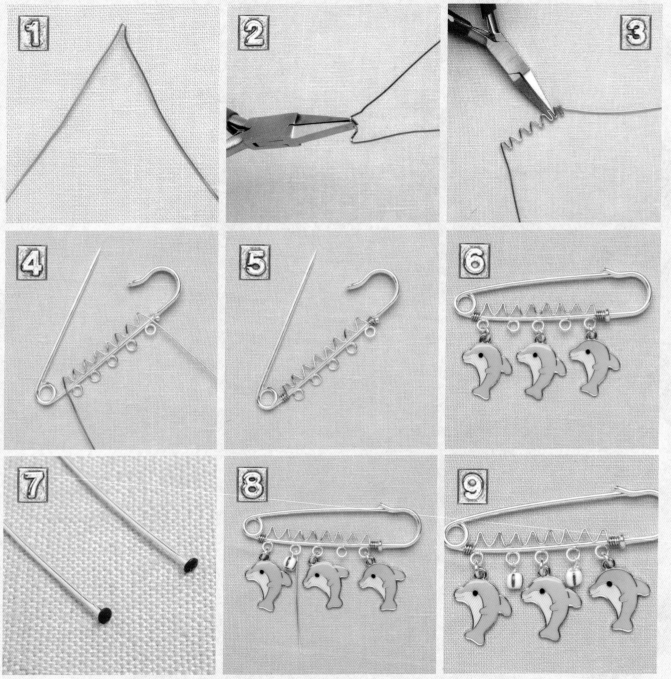

gecko

Use the art of beading
to give the classic
1920s lizard brooch
a modern twist!

Everything you will need...

To get a great geometric, scaly skin effect use bicone crystals rather than seed beads for this animal pattern.

1 1 x sew-on brooch pin

2 13 x 4mm light topaz bicone crystals

3 1 x 4mm peridot bicone crystal

4 9 x 6mm peridot bicone crystals

5 3 x 6mm light siam bicone crystals

6 28 x 6mm emerald bicone crystals

7 2 x 6mm jet bicone crystals

8 3ft 3in (1m) of US 28-gauge (SWG 30, 0.3mm) green beading wire

Side cutters

Needle

Green cotton thread

Scissors

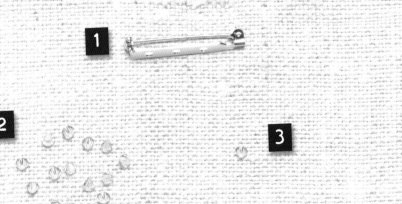

gecko

Bead map

Assembling gecko

1 If you have done bead work before then you can use the bead map illustrated above. Alternatively, thread one emerald bead halfway along the length of green beading wire. Bend the wire down either side of the bead so you have a left wire and a right wire of equal length. Add two emerald beads onto the left wire then thread the right wire through both beads in the opposite direction. Pull the wire so the three beads come together to form a small triangle.

2 Onto the left wire add: one jet bead, one emerald bead, and another jet bead. Again, thread the right wire through all three beads in the opposite direction and pull. You now have six beads all together in a triangle formation.

3 Thread onto the left wire two emerald beads and once more take the right wire and thread through both these two beads going in the opposite direction. Pull the wire to bring all the beads together and you have formed the head.

4 Take the left wire and thread on two emerald beads followed by three light topaz beads. Then thread the wire back through the two emerald beads going the other way. Gently pull the wire and you have formed one leg. Repeat this step to make the other leg on the right-hand wire.

5 Add onto the left wire: one emerald bead followed by one light siam bead, followed by a further emerald bead. Again, take the right wire and thread through all three beads going the opposite way and pull. This is now the first line of the body.

6 Keep adding the following formations onto the left wire and then threading the right wire back through the beads each time. For the next row, thread: one emerald bead, two larger peridot beads, and one emerald bead. For the following row thread: one larger peridot bead, one light siam bead, and one larger peridot bead. For the next row use: one emerald bead, two larger peridot beads, and one emerald bead. For the final body row, thread: one emerald bead, one light siam bead, and a last emerald bead.

7 Now the body is formed you need to make the other two legs. In the same way you made the previous legs, thread on two emerald beads followed by three light topaz beads on the left wire. Then thread the wire back through the two emerald beads going the other way. Repeat again to make the other leg on the right-hand wire.

8 Take two emerald beads and thread them onto the left wire. Again, thread the right wire through both beads going in the opposite direction and pull so the beads fit snugly together.

9 To make the tail add onto the left wire one emerald bead and then thread the right wire through the bead the opposite way. Continue this process, alternating the emerald and larger peridot beads until they are all used. Now add the small peridot bead onto the left wire, threading the right wire through it the opposite way and finally the last light topaz bead. Twist the wires together, thread them back through the light topaz bead, and cut away excess wire. Sew the brooch pin onto the back using green cotton.

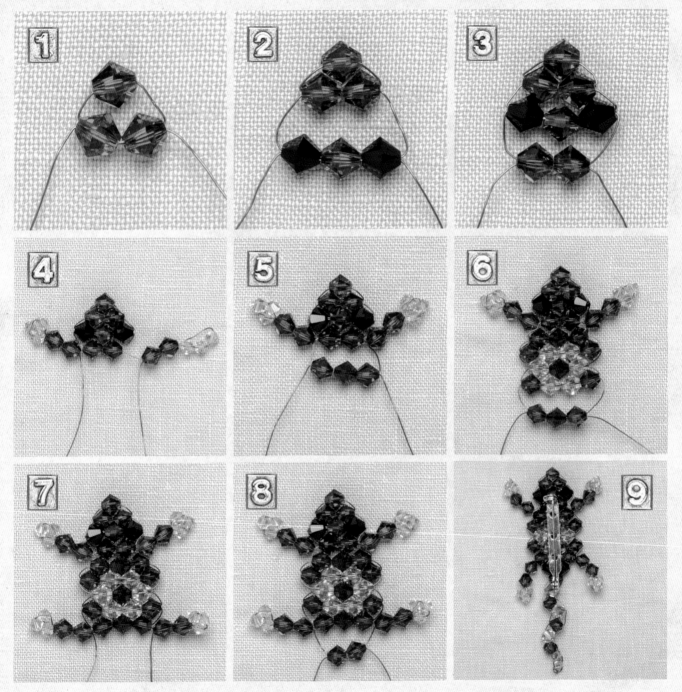

sonia

Hog the limelight with this prickly brooch
that will leave you bristling with pride!

Everything you will need...

Whether you take your inspiration from Beatrix Potter's Mrs Tiggy-Winkle or Sonic the Hedgehog, you'll have fun creating this cute brooch.

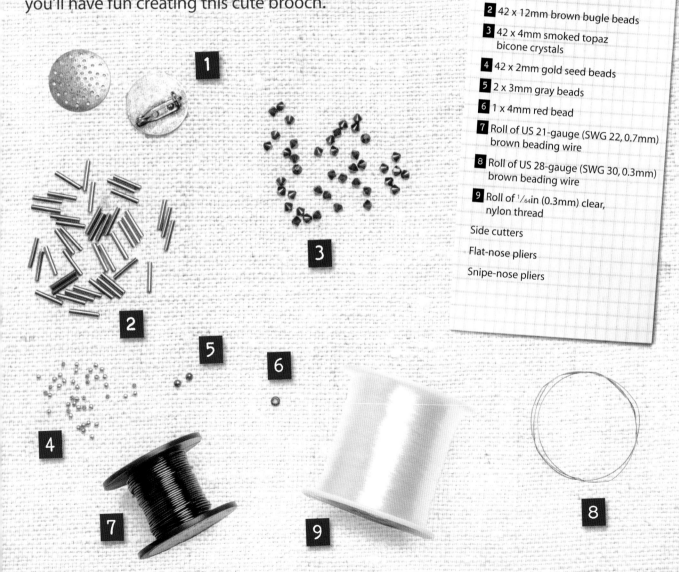

1. 1 x 1in (25mm) sieve and brooch back
2. 42 x 12mm brown bugle beads
3. 42 x 4mm smoked topaz bicone crystals
4. 42 x 2mm gold seed beads
5. 2 x 3mm gray beads
6. 1 x 4mm red bead
7. Roll of US 21-gauge (SWG 22, 0.7mm) brown beading wire
8. Roll of US 28-gauge (SWG 30, 0.3mm) brown beading wire
9. Roll of ¹⁄₆₄in (0.3mm) clear, nylon thread

Side cutters

Flat-nose pliers

Snipe-nose pliers

sonia

Assembling sonia

1 Cut 3ft 3in (1m) of the thicker brown wire from the roll. Thread 4in (100mm) of wire through a hole on the outer ring of holes on the sieve. Twist it together with the long end for $^5/_8$in (15mm) and then bend the long end back, threading it through the fourth hole along the outer ring.

2 Hold the smaller length of wire and bend it up at an angle toward the center of the sieve. Bend this length back down before it reaches the center hole, threading it through the hole between the middle of the triangle of wire already in place. Twist the now very small length back around the wire to form a triangle to give it some extra thickness. Cut away any excess wire.

3 Now take the remaining long piece of wire and start to wrap it around the three-dimensional triangle to form a nose. Try and keep the coils as even as possible. When you get to the tip of the nose add the red bead to the wire.

4 Continue to wrap the wire up and down the nose to create a solid cone. Finish your coils at the sieve end so you can poke the wire through a hole and bend it back on itself to secure it in place. Bend the cone up with your fingers at the end to make it curve upward slightly.

5 Thread two gray beads onto 8in (20cm) of the thinner beading wire. Slide them along so they are centered on the wire. Twist one of the beads a few times to secure it and then twist the second one $^3/_8$in (10mm) along.

6 Hold the gray beads onto the nose you completed earlier and start to wrap the remaining lengths of the thinner brown wire around it, weaving it between the eyes to fix them in place. Make sure you finish with the thin wires at the sieve end so you can twist them together and tuck any remaining wire down the inside of the nose.

7 Cut 3ft 3in (1m) of nylon thread and tie a large knot 2in (50mm) from one end. Thread the nylon through the central hole on the sieve so the knot rests against the concave surface of the sieve. Thread onto the nylon, one smoked topaz crystal, one brown bugle bead, and one gold seed bead. Then thread the nylon back through the bugle bead and crystal only. Thread the nylon back through the same hole and pull the thread tightly so all the beads rest snugly against the convex surface of the sieve.

8 Thread the nylon through the next hole along on the sieve and repeat the bead formation of one smoked topaz crystal followed by one brown bugle bead, and one gold seed bead. Then thread the nylon back through the bugle and crystal beads, and back through the same hole. Keep repeating this step until you have completed an entire ring of beads.

9 You will run out of nylon thread, so when you are near the end simply tie it to the long end of the knot and cut away any excess thread. Cut another 3ft 3in (1m) and again tie a knot 2in (50mm) from one end and thread it through the next hole along on the sieve. Keep repeating the threading pattern until you have used up all the available holes on the sieve. Finally, click the brooch back onto the sieve, squashing the locator clips over the sieve using a pair of snipe-nose pliers.

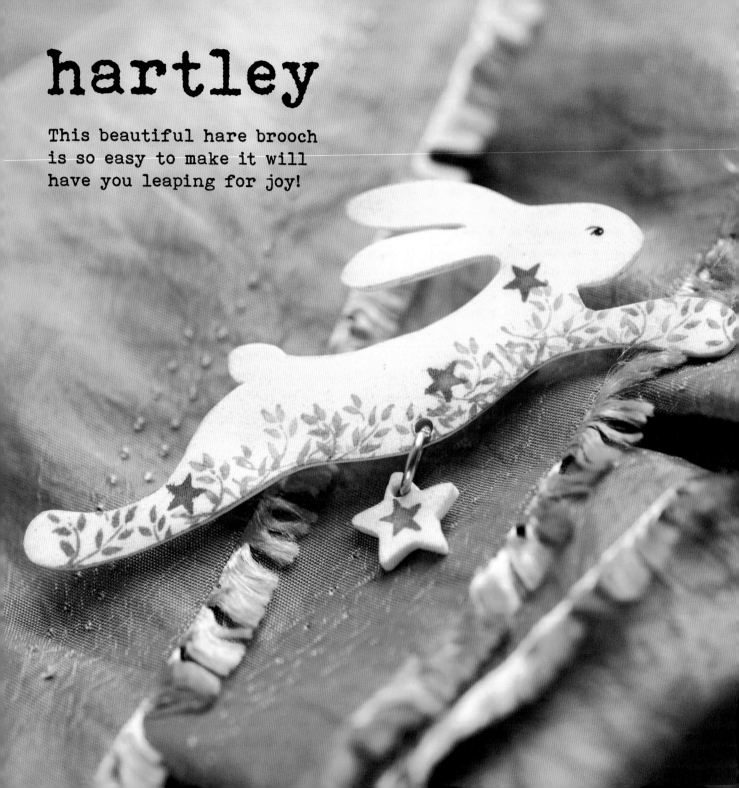

hartley

This beautiful hare brooch
is so easy to make it will
have you leaping for joy!

Everything you will need...

Experiment with using permanent felt-tip pens to color in your shapes on shrink plastic—giving you endless design possibilities.

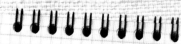

1 1 x sheet of US letter-size (A4) shrink plastic

2 1 x 1³/₁₆in (30mm) brooch pin

3 1 x 5mm green jumpring

Two-part adhesive

Scissors

Snipe-nose pliers

Flat-nose pliers

Eraser

Hole punch

Pencil

Permanent inks and stamp

1

2

3

Assembling hartley

1 Using a pencil, draw a leaping hare shape no larger than 6 x 4in (150 x 100mm) onto the matt side of a sheet of shrink plastic (see template on page 120). Remember that your design will shrink to a third of its size. Also, draw a star shape on the plastic and cut out both using scissors.

2 Take an eraser and rub out any pencil lines to leave clean, white shapes.

3 Punch a hole in the center at the bottom of your design and also at the top point of your star with a hole punch. The holes will also shrink during heating.

4 Now you can decorate your hare. I have used a rubber stamp and permanent waterproof ink for a professional finish but you can use permanent felt-tip pens if you prefer.

5 When the ink has dried, place your shape onto a flat baking tray and bake it in the oven following the manufacturer's instructions. It is best to do one shape at a time. The shape will twist and curl but then it will flatten out (see tip). Remove the plastic from the oven and allow it to cool.

6 Look at how the plastic has shrunk during the baking process!

7 Open the green jumpring and link it through the hole on the star charm and then link to the bottom of the hare's body and close.

8 Mix a small amount of two-part adhesive and stick the brooch pin onto the back of the hare and leave it to dry.

PLACE YOUR SHRINK PLASTIC SHAPES UNDER A HEAVY HARDBACK BOOK WHEN YOU TAKE THEM OUT OF THE OVEN TO ENSURE THEY COOL COMPLETELY FLAT.

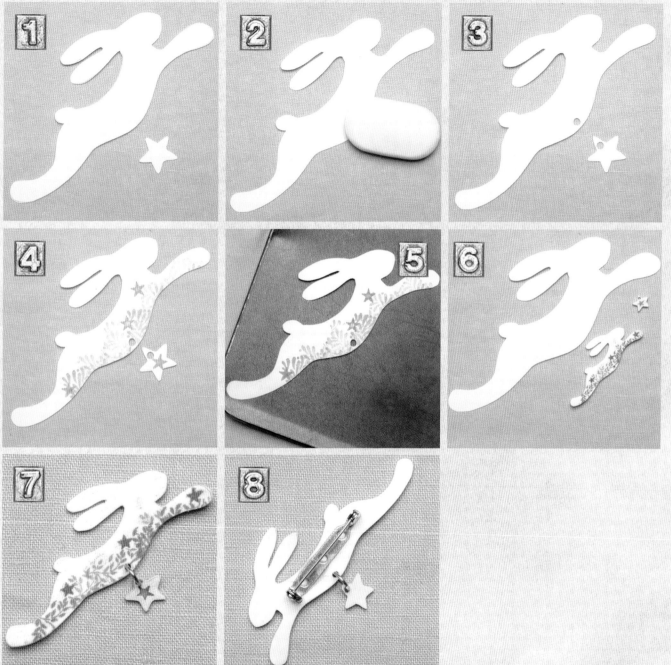

accessories

skye

This Victorian drawing of a stag
gives these cufflinks a vintage feel
and will make that special someone
feel like laird of the manor!

Everything you will need...

Make sure you coat your images on both sides in white (PVA) glue so the paper doesn't absorb the resin.

1. 2 x ¹¹/₁₆in (17mm) square-tray cufflink blanks
2. Pale-colored card
3. Two-part, pour-on, high-gloss resin

White (PVA) glue

Paint brush

Oil-based modeling clay (Plasticine)

Scissors

Mixing pots and sticks

1

2

3

skye

Assembling skye

1 Source an image of a stag's head from the Internet and scale it to size so it will fit inside the cufflink blank. Copy the image and then reverse it so you now have a pair of images. Print it out onto the pale colored card.

2 Cut out each image slightly smaller than $^{11}/_{16}$in (17mm) square so that they fit comfortably inside the cufflink blanks. Coat each image with white (PVA) glue back and front, then leave to dry.

3 Stick each image into the base of each cufflink blank, again using a small amount of white glue.

4 Prop each cufflink blank so the tray containing the image is completely horizontal. This is easily done using soft modeling clay, such as Plasticine.

5 High-gloss resins usually come in two parts: the actual resin and the hardener. Following the instructions on the packaging, mix equal parts of each thoroughly and pour the mixture into each tray of the cufflink blanks.

6 The consistency is very thick, so you can be generous with the amount you pour in because it does slightly shrink back when it cures. Blow lightly on the surface to pop the larger bubbles and leave to dry thoroughly.

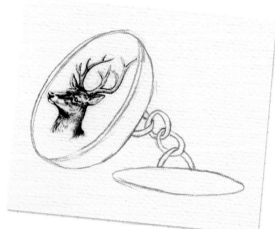

THINK ABOUT HOW TO 'PAIR' YOUR CHOSEN IMAGES FOR EACH CUFFLINK. SIMPLY REVERSE THEM FOR A SUBTLE DIFFERENCE.

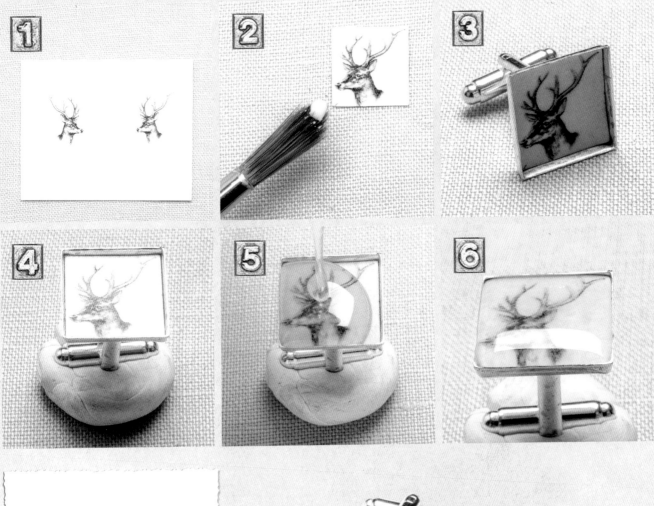

ANY SMALL
BUBBLES IN
YOUR RESIN WILL
DISAPPEAR AS
IT DRIES OUT.

flutterby

Wear summer in your hair with these beautiful
feather butterflies fluttering in your locks.

Everything you will need...

Using colors from the same palette combined with the same type of beads keeps this simple design sophisticated.

1 1 x 1ft 8in (500mm) length of US 28-gauge (SWG 30, 0.3mm) green beading wire

2 2 x feather butterflies

3 2 x Lucite leaves

4 8 x assorted Lucite flowers

5 8 x 2mm (size 10) seed beads

6 1 x wire hair comb

Side cutters

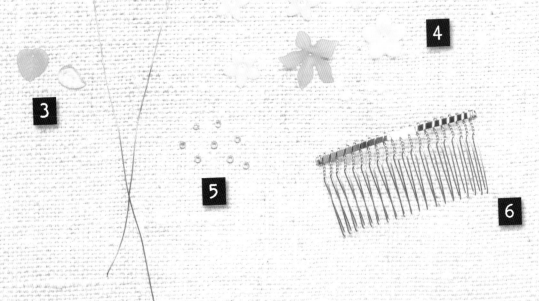

Assembling flutterby

1 Thread ³/₈in (10mm) of the end of the length of beading wire through the hole on a Lucite leaf. Bend it back on itself and twist together to form a stalk for the leaf.

2 Hold the leaf in position against a wire comb and start to wrap the long length of green beading wire around the top of the comb to secure the leaf in place.

3 Thread a small Lucite flower onto the wire followed by a seed bead. Then pass the wire back through the hole on the flower and wrap around the top of the comb. Continue to wrap the wire around the top of the comb, moving along it as you do so.

4 Continue to add different sizes and shapes of Lucite beads until you have covered the entire length of the hair comb.

5 Start to wrap the beading wire back along the comb heading towards the leaf where you first started to wrap it. This will secure everything in place and give you the opportunity to add some more flowers.

6 When you are back to where you started, thread another leaf onto the wire and again bend it back ³/₈in (10mm) and twist it to form another stem. Cut away any excess wire.

7 The feather butterflies come on long wires. Position your first butterfly against the comb and then start to tightly wrap the wire around the comb, weaving it between the flowers as you go.

8 Finally, add the last butterfly to the comb, wrapping the wire tightly around the top of the comb. Cut away excess wires from both butterflies.

ENSURE ANY ENDS OF WIRE ARE TUCKED UNDER SO THERE ARE NO SHARP POINTS LEFT STICKING OUT.

ribbit

You'll be jumping for joy
that this pretty frog
hopped onto your finger!

Everything you will need...

The simplicity of this wire-wrapped ring shows off this glass lamp-work frog bead beautifully.

1 1 x roll of US 21-gauge (SWG 22, 0.7mm) blue beading wire

2 1 x 20mm round, glass lamp-work frog bead

Side cutters

Ring mandrel

Snipe-nose pliers

Flat-nose pliers

Round-nose pliers

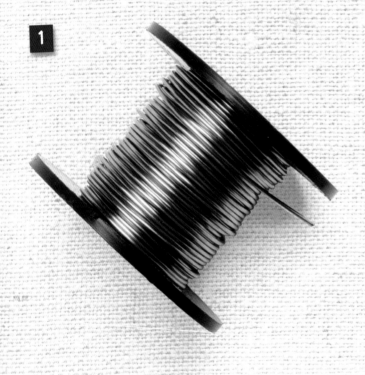

1

2

ribbit

Assembling ribbit

1 Cut 16in (405mm) of blue beading wire from the roll and thread through it the hole of the glass lamp-work frog bead. Center the bead on the wire.

2 Hold the frog bead on the ring mandrel at one size larger than your actual ring size. Bend the wire straight down either side of the bead.

3 Continue to bend both of the wires around the ring mandrel. Thread one end of wire back through the hole of the bead. Now thread the other end of wire through the other hole in the opposite direction.

4 Hold the end of each length of wire in a pair of flat-nose pliers and pull until the wires fit snugly around the ring mandrel. Keep threading and pulling the wire in this way until you can no longer fit the ends through the hole of your bead, with the wire finishing facing upwards.

5 Take the ring off the mandrel and start to coil the remaining ends of wire tightly around both side shanks of the ring. After several coils, cut the excess wire off using side cutters, ensuring you leave $^3/_8$in (10mm) of straight wire remaining.

6 Hold the end of the wire in the tip of your round-nose pliers and bend it to form a tight spiral. Lightly squash the spiral against the coils of wire you have just made on the ring shank.

7 The ring may have become a little misshapen at this point. Place it back on the mandrel to regain a perfect circular ring shape.

CUT LENGTHS OF WIRE LONGER THAN YOU REQUIRE—IT IS FAR EASIER TO MANIPULATE THEN CUT TO SIZE THAN WORK WITH A PIECE THAT IS A BIT SHORT.

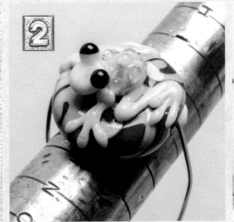

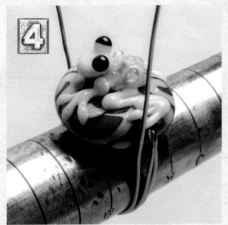

COLORED BEADING WIRE IS
EASIER TO USE THAN SILVER-PLATED
JEWELRY WIRE BECAUSE IT IS
MUCH SOFTER AND THEREFORE
EASIER TO MANIPULATE.

ribbit
- - - -

claudia

You shall go to the ladybug
ball with this fabulous
feather and bead fascinator!

Everything you will need...

There are endless possibilities with this design; experiment with different colored feathers for a variety of effects.

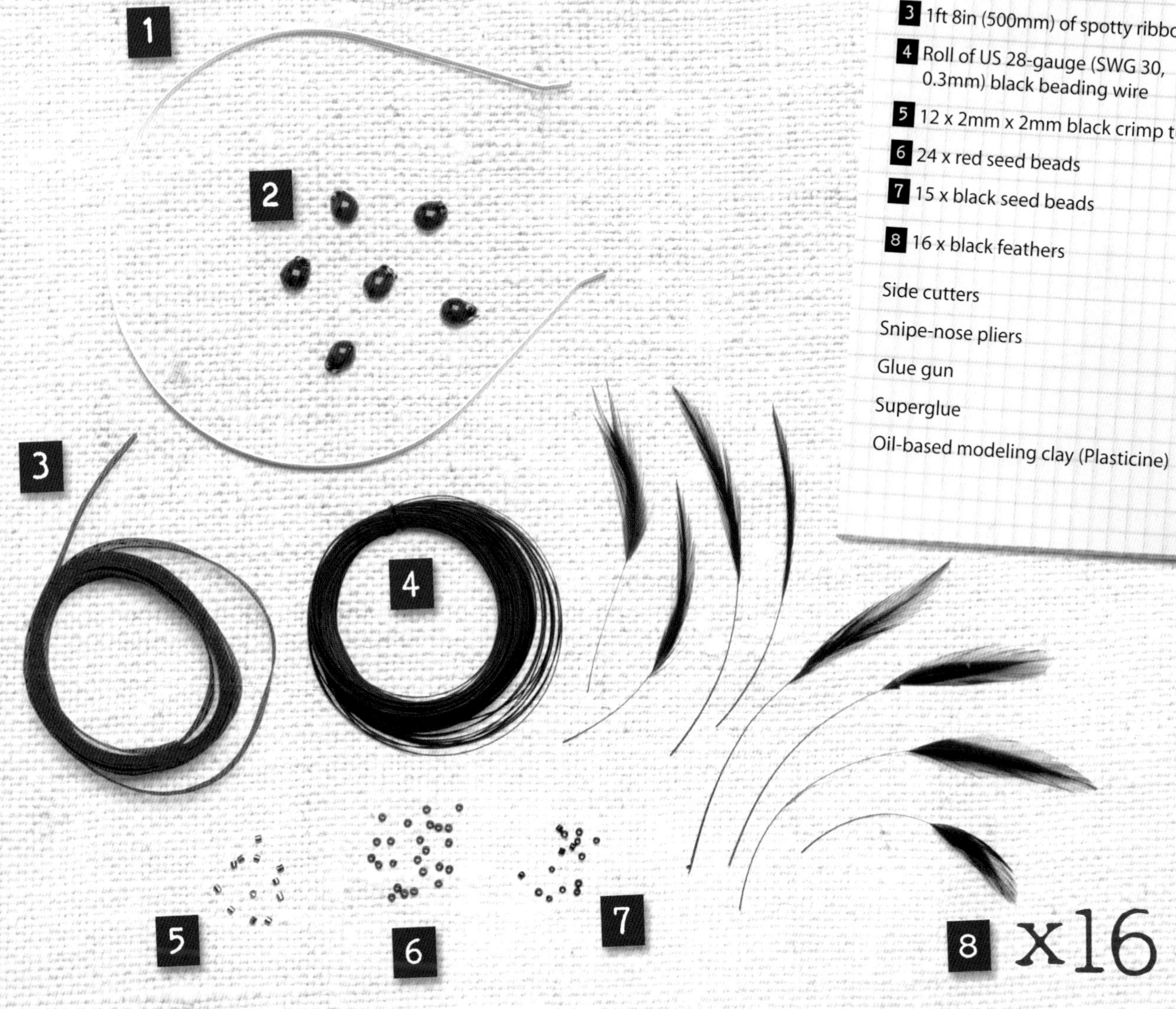

1 1 x thin, metal hair band

2 6 x 10mm ladybug beads

3 1ft 8in (500mm) of spotty ribbon

4 Roll of US 28-gauge (SWG 30, 0.3mm) black beading wire

5 12 x 2mm x 2mm black crimp tubes

6 24 x red seed beads

7 15 x black seed beads

8 16 x black feathers

Side cutters

Snipe-nose pliers

Glue gun

Superglue

Oil-based modeling clay (Plasticine)

1

2

3

4

5

6

7

8 x16

claudia

Assembling claudia

1 Cut 1ft 4in (400mm) of beading wire from the roll and hold it between your fingers at about 7in (180mm) from one end. At this point, start to wrap the wire tightly around the metal hair band slightly off-center. After a couple of coils make sure the other long end of wire, now also approximately 7in (180mm) long, is coming off the opposite side of the hair band from where you started.

2 Cut another two 1ft 4in (400mm) lengths of wire and wrap them in the same way so you have a group of six wires coiled around the hair band in one spot. Plug in your glue gun and allow it to heat up.

3 Take the black feathers and cut them so they are at least 4in (100mm) in length. Hold the feather by the quill and gently pinch the end of the quill between your thumbnail and index finger. The pulling action is much like curling gift ribbon and will make the quill have a good curve. You can add a few seed beads to some of the quills using a drop of superglue at each bead.

4 Stand the metal hair band in a lump of soft modeling clay (Plasticine) so it is secure and the group of wires that you wrapped on earlier are facing the top and are accessible to work on. Carefully add a tiny drop of melted glue from the glue gun onto the bottom of the quill on a feather and quickly hold it against the coils of black wire. Keep repeating this step, adding all of your feathers so they are evenly radiating from the coils.

5 Working on one wire at a time, cut each length so they are all approximately 6in (150mm) long. Again, hold the wire between your thumbnail and index finger and curl it. Add a tiny drop of superglue along the wire and add a red seed bead. Add three seed beads per wire, leaving at least 1¹⁄₂in (40mm) clear from each end.

6 Take a black crimp tube and squash it flat on the wire using snipe-nose pliers approximately 1¹⁄₄in (30mm) from the end of the wire. Add a ladybug bead and then another crimp tube. Again, squash the crimp tube flat as close to the top of the ladybug bead as possible, trapping it in place on the wire. Repeat this step to add ladybugs to all the wires.

7 Add another drop of superglue to the end tip of the wire and glue a red seed bead right at the end. Repeat this step, adding red seed beads to the ends of all of the wires.

8 Cut 8in (200mm) of beading wire and at the center point, tie a double bow onto it using your spotty ribbon. The overall size of the bow can be as large as you like. Cut the ends of the bow so you have pointed tails.

9 Hold the bow as firmly as possible against all of the wires and feathers to conceal the glue and wire where it all joins to the hair band. Neatly coil the long ends of wire that run through the bow around the metal band at either end. Cut away any excess wire.

templates

renard

hartley

resources

UK

Ang's Attic
Unit 12
North Norfolk Business Centre
Crossdale Street
Northrepps
NR27 9RQ
Tel: +44 (0)1263 516899
www.angs-attic.co.uk

BeadAddict
8 Charter Close
Sale
Cheshire
M33 5YG
Tel: +44 (0)161 973 1945
www.beadaddict.co.uk

Bead Aura
3 Neals Yard
Covent Garden
London
WC2H 9DP
Tel: +44 (0)20 7836 3002
www.beadaura.co.uk

Beadworks Bead Shop
21a Tower Street
Covent Garden
London
WC2H 9NS
Tel: +44 (0)20 7240 0931
www.beadshop.co.uk

Big Bad Beads
The Old Sunday School
Cape Cornwall Street
St Just
Cornwall
TR19 7JZ
www.bigbadbeads.co.uk

Bijoux Beads
2 Abbey Street
Bath
BA1 1NN
Tel: +44 (0)1225 482024
www.bijouxbeads.co.uk

Cookson Precious Metals Ltd
59–83 Vittoria Street
Birmingham
B1 3NZ
Tel: +44 (0)845 100 1122
www.cooksongold.com

JillyBeads Ltd
1 Anstable Road
Morecambe
LA4 6TG
Tel: +44 (0)1524 412728
www.jillybeads.co.uk

Needabeadonline
Unit 4a
Station Yard
Bawtry
Doncaster
South Yorkshire
DN10 6QD
Tel: +44 (0)1302 714774
www.needabeadonline.co.uk

Palmer Metals
401 Broad Lane
Coventry
CV5 7AY
Tel: +44 (0)845 644 9343
www.palmermetals.co.uk

Plush Addict Ltd
Unit 2
Enterprise Way
Edenbridge
Kent
TN8 6EW
Tel: +44 (0)845 519 4422
www.plushaddict.co.uk

Serendipity Beads
Crosshands
Carmarthenshire
SA14 6NT
Tel: +44 (0)1269 832238
www.serendipity-beads.co.uk

Shiney Company
5 Saville Row
Bath
BA1 2QP
Tel: +44 (0)1225 332506
www.shineyrocks.co.uk

Yum Yum Beads
3 Thorntons Arcade
Leeds
LS1 6LQ
Tel: +44 (0)113 244 2888
www.yumyumbeads.co.uk

USA

Auntie's Beads
5928 Hightower Drive
Watauga
Texas 76148
Tel: +1 866-26-BEADS
www.auntiesbeads.com

Beadshop.com
555 Bryant St. #293
Palo Alto
California 94301
Tel: +1 650-386-6962
www.beadshop.com

Beads of Paradise
16 E 17th St
New York
NY 10003
Tel: +1 212-620-0642
www.beadsofparadisenyc.com

Be Dazzled Beads
718 Thompson Lane
Nashville
Tennessee 37204
Tel: +1 615-292-0610
www.landofodds.com

D & I Beads
5350 W. Bell Rd #136
Glendale
Arizona 85308
Tel: +1 602-564-2900

www.dibeads.com
Fire Mountain Gems and Beads
One Fire Mountain Way
Grants Pass
Oregon 97526-2373
Tel: +1 800-355-2137
www.firemountaingems.com

Halstead Bead Inc.
6650 Inter-cal Way
Prescott
Arizona 86301
Tel: +1 800-528-0535
www.halsteadbead.com

Kazuri Beads USA
1861 Echo Lane
Lincoln
California 95648
www.kazuribeadsusa.com

Michaels
607 Broadway
Saugus
Massachusetts 01906
Tel: +1 781-233-3423
(Stores nationwide)
www.michaels.com

MKBeads
618 SW 3rd Street #150
Cape Coral
Florida 33991
Tel: +1 239-634-2232
Email: sales@mkbeads.com
www.mkbeads.com

Potomac Bead Company
100 South Main Street
Chambersburg, PA 17201
Tel: +1 717-491-1801
www.potomacbeads.com

Shipwreck Beads
8560 Commerce Place Drive NE
Lacey
Washington 98516
Tel: +1 800-950-4232
www.shipwreckbeads.com
Sunshine Discount Crafts
12335 62nd Street North
Largo
Florida 33773-3715
Tel: +1 800-729-2878
www.sunshinecrafts.com

acknowledgments

I would like to say thank you to all my family and friends and to you, the readers, who I hope are inspired to be creative. Long may it last! Finally, I would like to say thank you to all the staff at GMC Publications for giving me this opportunity to write my third book.

picture credits

Florida Memory: JJS0370 (p3 top right, p31 center bottom); JJS0406 (p5 top right, p85 top left) **George Eastman House**: 1971:0145:0001 (p30 center bottom, p124 bottom right) **iStock/Thinkstock**: lion (p2, p67) **Smithsonian Institution**: SIA2011-1235 (p66 center left); SIA2012-4383 (p103 bottom left); **State Library of New South Wales**: by Sam Hood (p2 top right, p48 top left) **State Library Queen Island**: Charmain Bernays dressed in rabbit costume (p1 bottom left, p84 center left) **The U.S. National Archive**s: 412-DA-2411 (p66 centre bottom); 412-DA-794 (p3 center, p49 center left)

about the author

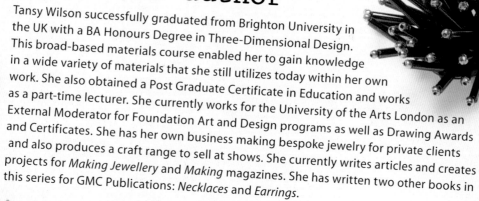

Tansy Wilson successfully graduated from Brighton University in the UK with a BA Honours Degree in Three-Dimensional Design. This broad-based materials course enabled her to gain knowledge in a wide variety of materials that she still utilizes today within her own work. She also obtained a Post Graduate Certificate in Education and works as a part-time lecturer. She currently works for the University of the Arts London as an External Moderator for Foundation Art and Design programs as well as Drawing Awards and Certificates. She has her own business making bespoke jewelry for private clients and also produces a craft range to sell at shows. She currently writes articles and creates projects for *Making Jewellery* and *Making* magazines. She has written two other books in this series for GMC Publications: *Necklaces* and *Earrings*.

index

To place an order, or request
a catalog, contact:

GMC Publications Ltd
Castle Place, 166 High Street,
Lewes, East Sussex, BN7 1XU
United Kingdom

Tel: +44 (0)1273 488005

www.gmcbooks.com